Speaking and Li[stening]
Activities
for the Early Years

Promoting Communication Skills Across the Foundation Stage Curriculum

Debbie Chalmers

Brilliant
PUBLICATIONS

We hope you enjoy using this book. If you would like further information on other books or e-resources published by Brilliant Publications, please write to the address given below or look on our website: www.brilliantpublications.co.uk.

Foundation Blocks series
Communication and Language with Literacy
Physical Development with Expressive Arts and Design
Personal, Social and Emotional Development with Understanding the World and Mathematics

Activities for 3–5 Year Olds series
All About Us
Caring and Sharing
Colours
Families
Food
Gardening
Pets
Shopping
Water
Weather

Other titles
Drama Activities for the Early Years
Phonic Limericks
Play Activities for the Early Years
Science and Technology for the Early Years
Creative Activities for the Early Years
Games for the Early Years
Preschool Art: It's the process not the product!

Published by Brilliant Publications
Unit 10
Sparrow Hall Farm
Edlesborough
Dunstable
Bedfordshire
LU6 2ES, UK

E-mail: info@brilliantpublications.co.uk
Website: www.brilliantpublications.co.uk
Tel: 01525 222292

© Text Debbie Chalmers 2014
© Design Brilliant Publications 2014
Printed book ISBN 978-1-78317-123-1
E-book ISBN 978-1-78317-124-8

First printed in the UK in 2015

Written by Debbie Chalmers
Illustrated by Brilliant Publications

Contents

Activities

Activity	Page no	Early Learning Goals Addressed						
		CL	PSED	PD	L	M	UW	EAD
Listening skills for 2-3 year olds								
Explanation of the development of listening skills in children aged 2-3 years								
Come outside	15	✔	✔	✔			✔	
Stop – Go!	16	✔	✔				✔	✔
Step over here	17	✔	✔	✔		✔		
Who made that noise?	18	✔	✔					✔
Body work	19	✔	✔	✔		✔		✔
Who said that?	20	✔	✔	✔				✔
Pass it to me	21	✔	✔			✔	✔	✔
Contrasts	22	✔	✔	✔				✔
Noisy stories	23	✔	✔		✔		✔	✔
Move in time	24	✔	✔	✔				✔
Tidy up time!	25	✔	✔	✔		✔		✔
Listening skills for 4-5 year olds								
Explanation of the development of listening skills in children aged 4-5 years								
Do it to order	27	✔	✔	✔		✔		✔
Please join in	28	✔	✔	✔		✔		✔
Make a sound story	29	✔	✔					✔
Shake and guess	30	✔	✔					✔
Find the sound	31	✔	✔				✔	✔
What's hiding?	32	✔	✔					✔
Put us together	33	✔	✔				✔	✔
Sequence of moves	34	✔	✔	✔		✔		
Who's talking?	35	✔	✔		✔		✔	
Sound mixing	36	✔	✔	✔				✔
Up and down	37	✔	✔	✔		✔		✔
Speaking skills for 2-3 year olds								
Explanation of the development of speaking skills in children aged 2-3 years								
May I have it please?	39	✔	✔	✔				
Yes or no?	40	✔	✔				✔	
Hello and goodbye	41	✔	✔			✔	✔	✔
Is it my turn now?	42	✔	✔					
Tell us what you did	43	✔	✔		✔	✔	✔	

Activity	Page no	Early Learning Goals Addressed						
		CL	PSED	PD	L	M	UW	EAD
Take your turn	44	✔	✔		✔		✔	
Choose your favourites	45	✔	✔				✔	
I need to go	46	✔	✔	✔			✔	✔
Who cares for you?	47	✔	✔				✔	
All join in	48	✔	✔	✔				✔
What if?	49	✔	✔	✔		✔	✔	
How old are we?	50	✔	✔			✔	✔	
Feelings	51	✔	✔				✔	✔
Story emotions	52	✔	✔	✔	✔			✔
Speaking skills for 4-5 year olds								
Explanation of the development of speaking skills in children aged 4-5 years								
What are they doing?	54	✔	✔		✔			
Thank you for coming	55	✔	✔	✔	✔		✔	✔
Find the rhymes	56	✔	✔	✔	✔		✔	✔
Round of sounds	57	✔	✔	✔	✔		✔	
Add a description	58	✔	✔				✔	
Will you be my friend?	59	✔	✔				✔	
Share with me	60	✔	✔					✔
Cycles of change	61	✔	✔		✔		✔	✔
What is happening?	62	✔	✔		✔	✔	✔	✔
Would you rather?	63	✔	✔				✔	
Sorry!	64	✔	✔				✔	✔
What did they do?	65	✔	✔	✔	✔		✔	✔
Hear the sound	66	✔	✔		✔			
Model speeches	67	✔	✔	✔	✔		✔	✔
How speaking and listening skills contribute to the overall development of children aged 2-5 years								
Prime area of Communication and Language	68–69							
Prime area of Personal, Social and Emotional Development	69–71							
Prime area of Physical Development	71–73							
Specific area of Expressive Arts and Design	73–74							
Specific area of Literacy	74–75							
Specific area of Understanding the World	75–77							
Specific area of Mathematics	77–78							
Speaking and listening skills for 2-3 year olds								
Listen to each other	79	✔	✔				✔	
Me please!	80	✔	✔	✔				✔
Which one do I mean?	81	✔	✔	✔			✔	

Activity	Page no	Early Learning Goals Addressed						
		CL	PSED	PD	L	M	UW	EAD
What happened to you?	82	✔	✔		✔		✔	
If I feel cross	83	✔	✔	✔				✔
Find it	84	✔	✔			✔		
I like that	85	✔	✔				✔	
Give me an answer	86	✔	✔	✔			✔	✔
Count the beats	87	✔	✔	✔		✔		
Catch the ball	88	✔	✔	✔		✔		✔
Speaking and listening skills for 4-5 year olds								
Hobbies	89	✔	✔				✔	
Name the instrument	90	✔	✔					✔
This is my story	91	✔	✔		✔			✔
Which way to go?	92	✔	✔	✔			✔	
Tell me a joke	93	✔	✔		✔	✔		✔
I wonder why	94	✔	✔	✔	✔		✔	✔
What am I doing?	95	✔	✔	✔				✔
Hello everybody	96	✔	✔			✔	✔	✔
Look what I can do	97	✔	✔	✔			✔	✔
My letter	98	✔	✔		✔			✔

Introduction

The development of language and the ability to communicate effectively is an important milestone. Although acquiring speaking and listening skills may be considered cognitive learning, they only develop fully when children share a social connection and understanding with people who care about them. Children need access to positive language experiences within supportive environments. They learn vocabulary through meaningful communication when they know that their early use of language will be celebrated and encouraged.

Early years practitioners and teachers do not assume that children will develop confident and effective speaking and listening skills regardless of their earlier experiences, or underestimate the vital roles played by parents and other primary carers throughout their children's early years. They know that it is important to share an understanding of early language development and to show sensitivity in meeting each family's needs, in order to empower parents and carers and encourage them to build confident interactions with their children, as many children suffer long lasting effects if their early language, understanding and communication skills are less well developed from the age of two years.

Beginning with trials in pilot areas from 2006, the Department of Education introduced a programme of funded places for two year olds that reached every local authority by 2010. The scheme made the 20% most disadvantaged two year olds eligible for 15 hours of free early education per week from September 2013, and the scheme was expanded further, to include many more children, from September 2014. All three and four year olds are already entitled to fifteen hours of early education per week. Many of the two year olds taking up funded places may have had early experiences and family circumstances that did not provide typical stimulation and some will present behavioural or learning challenges. Warm and responsive practitioners need to meet these children's individual needs by promoting early communication skills, such as making eye contact, directing and focusing attention and turn taking, and sitting close to them to engage in conversation.

Children aged from two years to four and a half years attending a setting together will be at very different stages of verbal communication. The two year olds, and even some of the three year olds, may be only just beginning to string words together, while some of the four year olds will be capable of deep and involved conversations that include descriptions, sequences, memories, predictions, discussions and negotiations.

Encouraging all of the children to talk and supporting and extending their developing verbal skills will allow them to learn from each other. The younger ones may acquire new vocabulary, greater fluency and an understanding of persuasion, negotiation and compromise, while the older ones may develop patience, empathy and the ability to express themselves simply and clearly.

All children may learn good manners and co-operation skills and form friendships with adults and with each other, as they learn to speak confidently and politely and to listen to and consider what others have to say. Well-developed speaking and listening skills promote teamwork and sensitivity and allow children to gradually take a greater responsibility for their own needs, as well as to learn through their play as they describe, discuss, plan, wonder, pretend and imagine.

The activities in this book are intended to form a practical resource for practitioners to use whenever they need ideas to offer specific extra support or practice in speaking and listening skills to the children in their care.

Through carefully planned and supported games

and activities, practitioners may encourage children to learn and practise vital skills in speaking and listening, such as:

- ❖ expressing their own needs and feelings and understanding the needs and feelings of others
- ❖ sharing and taking turns
- ❖ asking to join in with play and inviting others to join them
- ❖ negotiating and reaching compromises in order to play successfully with others
- ❖ developing imaginative narratives, characters and scenarios in small-world and role-play
- ❖ learning new vocabulary and grammar and using richer and more complicated language
- ❖ describing their own ideas and experiences
- ❖ sharing their home languages and cultures with the group
- ❖ understanding reasons and timescales in order to tolerate delay or postponement of gratification
- ❖ verbalising emotions, especially anger or distress, in order to maintain control
- ❖ taking part in conversations and discussions with an adult, a friend or a group
- ❖ knowing when to be silent and give attention to others in order to learn
- ❖ respecting others' right to speak and waiting or joining in appropriately
- ❖ enjoying a variety of stories, poems, rhymes and songs
- ❖ recognising and matching rhymes, alliteration and phonic sounds
- ❖ developing rhythm and fluency in speech and using intonation to express meaning
- ❖ absorbing and exchanging information
- ❖ asking, understanding and explaining why things happen and how things work
- ❖ predicting what might happen and understanding risks and consequences of actions

- ❖ using appropriate speech in different situations in order to communicate effectively with families, with friends, with familiar carers and teachers, with strangers or within a group
- ❖ using polite speech and good manners in order to express their needs and wishes clearly
- ❖ developing self-confidence through the knowledge that they can communicate effectively with others whenever they need to
- ❖ being aware of the world around them and alert to both opportunities and dangers
- ❖ making the most of every possible experience for fun and learning
- ❖ forming satisfying and constructive relationships with adults and peers.

Rough age guides are given for ease of grouping the ideas within the book, but all activities may be adapted by practitioners to suit children at any age or stage of development. They can be used on a one-to-one basis with a child, or with a small group, a larger group or the whole group at the setting, provided enough practitioners are available to maintain an appropriate adult to child ratio, and can be extended as dictated by the children's needs and abilities. Adults should lead and support the children when first introducing activities, but encourage them to go on to use them in their own play and daily lives once they are confident, in order to further develop the ideas and consolidate the skills learned.

Learning opportunities and links to the early learning goals of the revised EYFS are clearly listed at the end of each activity, to assist in the recognising, assessing and recording of children's progress and development.

Learning opportunities linked to Early Learning Goals

All of the activities contribute to children's development towards the Early Learning Goals in the prime areas of Communication and Language and Personal, Social and Emotional Development. The other prime and specific areas of development vary between the activities.

Individual children will be achieving at different levels, even within small groups, and practitioners should record their progress using their own observations and professional judgement. Children may arrive at a setting with skills well below what might usually be expected according to their chronological age, but they may go on to achieve a high level of development and progress. A list of the learning opportunities and developmental stepping stones that it may be appropriate to record, from 8-20 months to 40-60+ months, is therefore given, allowing practitioners to select different and appropriate statements for each child.

To ensure that all of the possible learning opportunities and developmental stepping stones will fit into the space available on each activity page, a system of numbers is used. Practitioners should refer to the following key when recording progress and development, until they become familiar with the statements and their numbers.

Developmental stepping stones - key to numbers used:

Communication and Language - Listening and attention (CL-LA)

1. Listens to and enjoys rhythmic patterns in rhymes and stories (16–26 months).
2. Enjoys rhymes and demonstrates listening by trying to join in with actions or vocalisation (16–26 months).
3. Recognises and responds to many familiar sounds (22–36 months).
4. Shows interest in play with sounds, songs and rhymes (22–36 months).
5. Single channelled attention – responds to own name when spoken by a familiar adult (22–36 months).
6. Listens to others one-to-one or in small groups when conversation interests them (30–50 months).
7. Listens to stories with increasing attention and recall (30–50 months).
8. Joins in with repeated refrains and anticipates key events and phrases in rhymes and stories (30–50 months).
9. Focuses attention on one person speaking or one sound at a time (30–50 months).
10. Is able to follow directions (30–50 months).
11. Maintains attention, concentrates and sits quietly during appropriate activity (40–60+ months).

Communication and Language - Understanding (CL-U)

1. Selects familiar objects by name and will go to find objects when asked, or will identify objects from a group (16–26 months).
2. Understands simple sentences (16–26 months).
3. Understands more complex sentences (22–36 months).
4. Understands simple questions (22–36 months).
5. Develops understanding of simple concepts (22–36 months).
6. Understands uses of objects (30–50 months).
7. Shows understanding of prepositions by carrying out actions (30–50 months)
8. Responds to simple instructions (30–50 months).
9. Responds to instructions involving a two-part sequence (40–60+ months).
10. Understands humour, such as nonsense rhymes and jokes (40–60+ months).

11. Listens and responds to ideas expressed by others in conversation or discussion (40–60+ months).

Communication and Language - Speaking (CL-S)

1. Begins to put two words together (16–26 months).
2. Uses different types of everyday words, including nouns, verbs and adjectives (16–26 months).
3. Begins to talk about people and things that are not present (16–26 months).
4. Uses language as a powerful means of widening contacts and sharing feelings, experiences and thoughts (22–36 months).
5. Learns new words very rapidly and is able to use them in communicating (22–36 months).
6. Uses gestures, sometimes with limited talk (22–36 months).
7. Uses a variety of questions (22–36 months).
8. Begins to use more complex sentences to link thoughts (30–50 months).
9. Can retell a simple past event in a correct order (30–50 months).
10. Uses talk to connect ideas, explain what is happening and anticipate what might happen next, recall and relive past experiences (30–50 months).
11. Questions why things happen and gives explanations (30–50 months).
12. Uses a range of tenses (30–50 months).
13. Uses intonation, rhythm and phrasing to make meanings clear to others (30–50 months).
14. Uses vocabulary focused on objects and people of particular importance (30–50 months).
15. Builds up vocabulary that reflects a breadth of experiences (30–50 months).
16. Extends vocabulary, especially by grouping and naming, exploring the meanings and sounds of new words (40–60+ months).
17. Uses language to imagine and recreate roles and experiences in play situations (40–60+ months).
18. Links statements and sticks to a main theme or intention (40–60+ months).
19. Uses talk to organise, sequence and clarify thinking, ideas, feelings and events (40–60+ months).
20. Introduces a storyline or narrative into their play (40–60+ months).
21. Expresses self effectively, showing awareness of listeners' needs and observing manners and social conventions (40–60+ months).

Personal, Social and Emotional Development - Making relationships (PSED-MR)

1. Interacts with others and explores new situations when supported by a familiar person (8-20 months).
2. Plays alongside others (16–26 months).
3. Interested in others' play and starting to join in (22–36 months).
4. Seeks out others to share experiences (22–36 months).
5. Directs attention for group participation and can play in a group, extending and elaborating play ideas (30–50 months).
6. Initiates play, offering cues to peers to join them (30–50 months).
7. Keeps play going by responding to what others are saying or doing (30–50 months).
8. Demonstrates friendly behaviour, initiating conversations and forming good relationships with peers and familiar adults (30–50 months).
9. Initiates conversations, attends to and takes account of what others say (40–60+ months).
10. Explains own knowledge and understanding and asks appropriate questions of others (40–60+ months).
11. Takes steps to resolve conflicts with other children, such as finding a compromise (40–60+ months).

Personal, Social and Emotional Development Self-confidence and self-awareness (PSED-SCSA)

1. Expresses own preferences and interests (22–36 months).
2. Can select and use activities and resources with help (30–50 months).
3. Welcomes and values praise for actions and achievements (30–50 months).
4. Enjoys the responsibility of carrying out small tasks (30–50 months).

5. Is more outgoing towards unfamiliar people and more confident in new social situations (30–50 months).
6. Is confident to talk to other children when playing and will communicate freely about own home and community (30–50 months).
7. Shows confidence in asking adults for help (30–50 months).
8. Is confident to speak to others about own needs, wants, interests and opinions (40–60+ months).
9. Can describe self in positive terms and talk about abilities (40–60+ months).

Personal, Social and Emotional Development - Managing feelings and behaviour (PSED-MFB)

1. Begins to understand 'yes', 'no' and some boundaries (8-20 months).
2. Responds to a few appropriate boundaries with encouragement and support (22–36 months).
3. Seeks comfort from familiar adults when needed (22–36 months).
4. Can express own feelings such as happy, sad, cross, scared and worried (22–36 months).
5. Responds to the feelings and wishes of others (22–36 months).
6. Shows understanding of and co-operates with some boundaries and routines (22–36 months).
7. Can inhibit own actions and behaviours (22–36 months).
8. Is aware of own feelings and knows that some actions and words can hurt others' feelings (30–50 months).
9. Begins to accept the needs of others and can take turns and share resources, sometimes with support from others (30–50 months).
10. Can usually tolerate delay when needs are not immediately met and understands that wishes may not always be met (30–50 months).
11. Can usually adapt behaviour to different events, social situations and changes in routine (30–50 months).
12. Understands that own actions affect other people (40–60+ months).
13. Is aware of the boundaries set and of behavioural expectations in the setting (40–60+ months).

14. Begins to be able to negotiate and solve problems without aggression (40–60+ months).

Physical Development - Moving and handling (PD-MH)

1. Shows control in holding and using items such as jugs for pouring, hammers, books and mark making tools (22–36 months).
2. Moves freely and with pleasure and confidence in a range of ways (30–50 months).
3. Runs skilfully and negotiates space successfully, adjusting speed or direction to avoid obstacles (30–50 months).
4. Uses one-handed tools and equipment (30–50 months).
5. Can copy some letters (30–50 months).
6. Experiments with different ways of moving (40–60+ months).
7. Negotiates space successfully when playing racing and chasing games with other children, adjusting speed or changing direction to avoid obstacles (40–60+ months).
8. Handles tools, objects, toys, instruments, construction and malleable materials safely and with increasing control (40–60+ months).
9. Begins to form recognisable letters (40–60+ months).

Physical Development - Health and self-care (PD-HSC)

1. Begins to be independent in self-care, but still often needs adult support (22–36 months).
2. Can tell adults when hungry or tired or when they want to rest or play (30–50 months).
3. Shows some understanding that good practices with regard to exercise, eating, sleeping and hygiene can contribute to good health (40–60+ months).
4. Shows understanding of the need for safety when tackling new challenges and considers and manages some risks (40–60+ months).
5. Practises some appropriate safety measures without direct supervision (40–60+ months).

Speaking and Listening Activities for the Early Years

Expressive Arts and Design - Exploring and using media and materials (EAD-EUMM)

1. Imitates and improvises actions they have observed (8-20 months).
2. Begins to move to music and listen to or join in with rhymes or songs (16–26 months).
3. Joins in with the singing of favourite songs (22–36 months).
4. Creates sounds by banging, shaking, tapping or blowing (22–36 months).
5. Shows an interest in the way musical instruments sound (22–36 months).
6. Enjoys joining in with dancing and ring games (30–50 months).
7. Sings a few familiar songs (30–50 months).
8. Begins to move rhythmically (30–50 months).
9. Imitates movement in response to music (30–50 months).
10. Taps out simple repeated rhythms (30–50 months).
11. Explores and learns how sounds can be changed (30–50 months).
12. Begins to be interested in and describe the texture of things (30–50 months).
13. Begins to build a repertoire of songs and dances (40–60+ months).
14. Explores the different sounds of instruments (40–60+ months).
15. Uses simple tools and techniques competently and appropriately (40–60+ months).

Expressive Arts and Design - Being imaginative (EAD-BI)

1. Begins to make believe by pretending (22–36 months).
2. Creates movement in response to music (30–50 months).
3. Makes up rhythms (30–50 months).
4. Engages in imaginative role-play based on own first-hand experiences (30–50 months).
5. Initiates new combinations of movement and gesture in order to express and respond to feelings, ideas and experiences (40–60+ months).
6. Introduces a storyline or narrative into play (40–60+ months).
7. Plays alongside other children who are engaged in the same theme (40–60+ months).
8. Plays cooperatively as part of a group to develop and act out a narrative (40–60+ months).

Literacy - Reading (L-R)

1. Repeats words or phrases from familiar stories (22–36 months).
2. Fills in the missing word or phrase in a known rhyme, story or game (22–36 months).
3. Enjoys rhyming and rhythmic activities (30–50 months).
4. Shows awareness of rhyme and alliteration (30–50 months).
5. Recognises rhythm in spoken words (30–50 months).
6. Listens to and joins in with stories and poems, one-to-one and in small groups (30–50 months).
7. Joins in with repeated refrains and anticipates key events and phrases in rhymes and stories (30–50 months).
8. Begins to be aware of the way stories are structured (30–50 months).
9. Suggests how a story might end (30–50 months).
10. Listens to stories with increasing attention and recall (30–50 months).
11. Describes main story settings, events and principal characters (30–50 months).
12. Shows interest in illustrations and print in books (30–50 months).
13. Looks at books independently (30–50 months).
14. Holds books the correct way up and turns pages (30–50 months).
15. Uses vocabulary and forms of speech that are increasingly influenced by experiences of books (40–60+ months).
16. Enjoys an increasing range of books (40–60+ months).
17. Knows that information can be retrieved from books and computers (40–60+ months).

Literacy - Writing (L-W)

1. Ascribes meanings to marks seen in different places (30–50 months).
2. Gives meanings to marks made when drawing, writing and painting (40–60+ months).

© Debbie Chalmers and Brilliant Publications

3. Continues a rhyming string (40–60+ months).
4. Hears and says the initial sound in a word (40–60+ months).
5. Links sounds to letters, naming and sounding the letters of the alphabet (40–60+ months).
6. Writes own name and other things such as labels and captions (40–60+ months).
7. Attempts to write short sentences in meaningful contexts (40–60+ months).

Understanding the World - People and communities (UW-PC)

1. Enjoys pictures and stories about self, own family and other people (16–26 months).
2. Has a sense of own immediate family and relations (22–36 months).
3. In pretend play, imitates everyday actions and events from own family and cultural background (22–36 months).
4. Begins to form own friendships (22–36 months).
5. Learns about similarities and differences that connect people to and distinguish them from others (22–36 months).
6. Shows interest in the lives of familiar people (30–50 months).
7. Remembers and talks about significant events from own experiences (30–50 months).
8. Recognises and describes special times or events for family or friends (30–50 months).
9. Shows interest in different occupations and ways of life (30–50 months).
10. Knows some of the things that make people unique and can talk about some similarities and differences in relation to friends or family (30–50 months).

Understanding the World - The world (UW-W)

1. Knows things are used in different ways. (8–20 months).
2. Explores objects by linking together different approaches and using different senses. (16–26 months).
3. Enjoys playing with small-world models (22–36 months).
4. Notices detailed features of objects in the environment (22–36 months).

5. Can talk about some things observed, such as plants and animals or natural and found objects (30–50 months).
6. Talks about why things happen and how things work (30–50 months).
7. Shows care and concern for living things and the environment (30–50 months).

Understanding the World - Technology (UW-T)

1. Knows how to operate simple equipment, such as a CD player (30–50 months).
2. Shows an interest in technological real objects, such as cameras (30–50 months).
3. Shows skill in making toys work by pressing parts or lifting flaps to achieve effects such as sounds or movements (30–50 months).

Mathematics - Numbers (M-N)

1. Begins to organise and categorise objects (16–26 months).
2. Uses some language of quantities (22–36 months).
3. Uses some number names and number language spontaneously (30–50 months).
4. Uses some number names accurately in play (30–50 months).
5. Realises that not only objects, but anything, such as movements, can be counted (30–50 months).
6. Counts up to three or four objects by saying one number name for each item (40–60+ months).
7. Counts actions or objects which cannot be moved (40–60+ months).
8. Counts an irregular arrangement of up to ten objects (40–60+ months).

Mathematics - Shape, space and measure (M-SSM)

1. Associates a sequence of actions with daily routines (16–26 months).
2. Begins to use the language of size (22–36 months).
3. Understands some talk about immediate past and future (22–36 months).
4. Anticipates specific time based events such as

mealtimes or hometime (22–36 months).

5. Uses positional language (30–50 months).

6. Begins to talk about the shapes of everyday objects (30–50 months).

7. Begins to use mathematical names for 3D and 2D shapes (40–60+ months).

8. Selects a particular named shape (40–60+ months).

9. Can describe own position relative to another person or object (40–60+ months).

10. Orders two or three items by length or height (40–60+ months).

11. Orders two items by weight or capacity (40–60+ months).

12. Uses everyday language related to time (40–60+ months).

13. Orders and sequences familiar events (40–60+ months).

14. Measures short periods of time in simple ways (40–60+ months).

Explanation of the development of listening skills in children aged 2-3 years

This statement of age is only a rough guide, as all children are individuals and will acquire skills and develop abilities at different times and different rates.

Much will depend upon the experiences and stimulation that they receive before the age of two years and the environments and relationships provided by their homes and the early years settings that they attend.

However, children are likely to acquire skills more or less in the following order, at the pace that is right for them.

- Focusing on one sound that interests them or on one person speaking.

- Responding to own name when spoken by a familiar adult or family member.

- Directing attention for safety or group participation.

- Copying sounds made by others, using voice, body or musical instrument.

- Responding to the language spoken within the setting, as well as the one used at home, if different.

- Carrying out simple directions when requested by an adult.

- Understanding and remembering boundaries, routines and behavioural expectations.

- Responding to different types of music by moving in time, clapping, humming or singing along.

- Enjoying rhythmic patterns, repetitive sounds and favourite rhymes, songs and stories.

- Naming or describing sounds heard while playing indoors and outdoors.

- Drawing the attention of others to sounds and investigating their sources.

Come outside

Equipment and resources

The outdoor area of the setting (or a nearby park or wood). A ratio of one practitioner for each two or three children. A selection of noisy toys or similar items.

Activity

* Walk with the children to a quiet area outdoors and encourage them to stand or sit still and listen very hard. Talk about something that you can hear, then invite them to tell the group what they can hear, supporting them with prompts and clues as necessary.

* Move close to trees and listen for sounds such as leaves rustling in the wind, bird calls and the running of squirrels.

* Stand at the gate by the street or road and listen for passing cars and motorbikes, emergency sirens, drills, machines and tools at roadworks, people's voices, babies crying or dogs barking.

* Walk towards the door of the setting and listen to the sounds of voices and play activities inside. Ask an adult to ring the door bell or temporarily activate the smoke alarm.

* Invite the children to identify each sound and name it or describe it so that you can name it for them. Encourage them to remember the sounds and to talk about them again when they hear them on other occasions.

Extensions

* Explore this activity in different seasons and weather conditions and compare the sounds heard. More creatures, birds and buzzing insects may be heard in summer, while traffic may be heavier in winter. Everything sounds different in rainy conditions, when trees are dripping and the roads are wet. Strong winds can be noisy, while snow promotes silence.

* Invite children to make their own noises outdoors. They could stamp their feet on paths, gently shake branches to make tree leaves whisper, tap large stones together or drop small stones into puddles or ponds.

* Encourage children to discuss the different possible sources of some sounds. For example, a vehicle passing in the road could be a car, a van or a bus; a rustling in the leaves at the top of a tree could be caused by the movements of a bird, a squirrel or a cat.

* Ask another adult to stand behind the group and make sounds for them to guess. Try bouncing a ball, playing a drum, shaking bells, clapping hands and knocking down a tower of bricks. Then, if the adult speaks to the children, ask them to say who they think it is.

Learning objectives linked to Early Learning Goals

(See pages 8–13 for abbreviations.)
* CL–LA: 3, 6, 9
* CL–U: 4, 5, 11
* CL–S: 5, 16, 18
* PSED–MR: 4, 9, 10
* PD–MH: 2
* UW–W: 4, 5

Stop - Go!

Equipment and resources

A large clear space with a safe ground or floor surface for movement. One practitioner to lead the game and one or two more practitioners to play the game with the children. A CD of children's songs or music suitable for dance. A CD player.

Activity

* Play music quietly and invite the children to dance and move around the room. At intervals, call out a player's name, loudly enough to be heard above the music.

* When players hear their names, they should freeze. When all players are frozen, stop the music and praise them all. Practitioners should join in to model the dancing and freezing and support the children as they move and freeze.

* If children find it too difficult to freeze for more than a few seconds, ask them to freeze when they hear their names, but move again as soon as the next name is called.

Extensions

* Ask players to freeze temporarily, at different times, by listening carefully and following your instructions. Call out the names accompanied by Stop and Go, sometimes inviting a player to move again immediately and sometimes asking several to stop before inviting any to move again.

* Call out two or three names at a time and encourage those players to freeze together. You may then invite them to move again at separate times.

* Suggest that players stop dancing when they hear their names by sitting down, or turning around, or jumping on the spot, instead of freezing.

Learning objectives linked to Early Learning Goals

(See pages 8–13 for abbreviations.)
* CL–LA: 5, 9
* CL–U: 8
* PSED–SCSA: 3
* PD–MH: 2, 6
* EAD–BI: 2

Step over here

Equipment and resources

A large clear space with a safe ground or floor surface for movement. One practitioner to lead the game and one or two more practitioners to play the game with the children.

Activity

* Invite the players to stand in a line or a group. Stand, facing them, a short distance away. Call out one player's name at a time. Each time somebody hears their name, they should take one giant step towards you. When one or more players reach you, the group should rush to join them and turn around, while you walk back from them and begin the game again in another direction.

* Practitioners should encourage all children to be quiet and listen for each name as it is called out, to move only at their turn and to support and remind each other.

* Call out names equally but in varied orders, taking into account the different lengths of children's strides, to make the game close and exciting.

Extensions

* Speak the names very quietly or whisper them, so that children must listen very hard and make no sound themselves in order to play.

* Add other movements. For example, When you hear your name, make a big jump or three hops or six tiny tiptoe steps.

* Call out a name and a number each time. For example, Katie – two steps; James – four steps.

Learning objectives linked to Early Learning Goals

(See pages 8–13 for abbreviations.)
* CL–LA: 5, 9, 10
* PSED–MR: 3, 5
* PSED–MFB: 2, 9, 12
* PD–MH: 6
* M–N: 7

Who made that noise?

Equipment and resources
A clear safe space to sit in a circle. One practitioner to lead the game and possibly more practitioners to play the game with the children. Three small-world toy animals for each player, such as a pig, a cow and a sheep or a dog, a cat and a duck. (Each player must have the same animals.) Recorded animal sounds to match the toys (from a commercial CD or created while on a visit to a farm), or an adult who can make the sounds recognisably.

Activity
* Invite the children to sit together in a circle or group and give each player their three animals. Play or make the sounds in a random order, asking the players to pick up the correct animal and wave it in the air each time they hear its sound, then put it down again.

* At first, leave gaps of silence for thinking between each sound (or pause the CD). Gradually close the gaps to speed up the children's reaction times. Encourage all children to try to keep up, but offer support and ensure that they understand that mistakes don't matter, so that there is no fear of failure.

Extensions
* Use six or nine different types of animal and give different mixes of three to players, so that not everybody will hold up one every time they hear a sound.

* Use pictures or photographs of the animals to hold up, point to or cover, instead of actual figures to handle.

* Try the game with relevant pictures and any other sounds that you can make or find, such as those of jungle animals, vehicles, tools, weather or musical instruments.

* Ask an adult to make sounds with the body, such as clapping, stamping, clicking fingers, humming and whistling, and challenge children to copy them and make them too.

Learning objectives linked to Early Learning Goals
(See pages 8–13 for abbreviations.)
* CL–LA: 3, 11
* CL–U: 8
* PSED–MR: 5, 7
* EAD–BI: 7

Body work

Equipment and resources
A large clear space with a safe ground or floor surface for movement. One practitioner for each group of three or four children.

Activity
* Invite the children and practitioners to sit or stand in a group, allowing enough space around each person for them to move their arms and legs comfortably. Make sounds using the body, such as clapping, tapping knees with hands, tapping hands or feet on floor, clicking fingers and knocking knees together. (Few young children can achieve clicking fingers, but they love to try or pretend.)

* After each one, invite the group to copy the movement to make the sound. Then challenge them to make the sound more loudly, more softly, more quickly or more slowly. Practitioners should encourage children to think and move independently, supporting them by modelling appropriate movements once they have tried to create their own, rather than just demonstrating for them to copy.

Extensions
* Make two sounds together for the group to imitate, such as clapping hands and tapping feet on floor or clicking fingers and knocking knees.

* Make one sound after another and ask the group to make them in the same order, such as tapping knees three times, then clapping hands four times.

* Introduce a rhythm to be copied, such as: clap clap, stamp stamp, click click, tap knees.

Learning objectives linked to Early Learning Goals
(See pages 8–13 for abbreviations.)
* CL–LA: 3, 10, 11
* CL–U: 9
* PSED–MR: 3, 7
* PD–MH: 6
* EAD–EUMM: 1, 4, 10
* M–N: 5

Who said that?

Equipment and resources

A large clear space. Four practitioners to lead the game and possibly more practitioners to play the game with the children.

Activity

* One adult should stand in each corner of the room or outdoor space, while the children stand together as a group in the centre, with the support of one or two more adults there if necessary. Explain to the children that the idea of the game is to guess who is speaking as quickly as possible.

* The four practitioners should take turns to speak loudly and clearly, using statements such as: Hey, look over here! Do you know who this is? Where am I? I'm here everybody! Can you look this way? Can you hear me? Encourage the players to turn to face each speaker and point to them.

* Ensure that the speakers perform in a random order and not around in a square. They should call out enthusiastically, gradually increasing the pace until they are almost overlapping with each other, and not wait politely for each other to take turns.

Extensions

* Suggest that the practitioners face away from the group, so that the children cannot see them speaking, and ask the players to guess and point without the visual clues to check their accuracy.

* Ask the players to walk to each speaker instead of pointing. The adults can gradually increase the speed of the game by speaking straight after each other, without pausing, so that the children barely reach one person before rushing off to the next. This can cause much amusement.

* Invite each speaker to suggest a movement for the players to make as they move on again. Those who are listening carefully may then run, jump, hop, skip, tiptoe or walk backwards, instead of just walking, as soon as they hear the next speaker.

Learning objectives linked to Early Learning Goals

(See pages 8–13 for abbreviations.)
* CL–LA: 9, 10
* CL–U: 8
* PSED–MR: 1, 2, 3
* PD–MH: 2, 3, 6
* EAD–EUMM: 1

Speaking and Listening Activities for the Early Years

Pass it to me

Equipment and resources

A large clear space. One practitioner to lead the game and two or three more practitioners to play the game with the children. A selection of basic items (clean and dry or unused), such as: a plate, a cup, a straw, a box, a ball, a spoon, a fork, a hairbrush, a toothbrush and a pencil.

Activity

* Invite the children and adults to sit together in a circle and place all the items in the centre. Point to each item in turn and name it, encouraging the children to listen carefully and to join in with the names that they know.

* Ask one of the practitioners first: Please pass me the (spoon). Take the item when it is offered and say Thank you. Then ask each child and adult in turn, around the circle, to pass a different item to you. Select the items according to the confidence and abilities of individual children and the degree of challenge that you want to offer to each child.

* When there are only two or three items left, replace them all in the centre of the circle again and mix them up, to avoid the game becoming too simple or ending abruptly.

* Talk with the group about the sizes, shapes, weights and textures of the different objects, inviting children to compare them and to describe how they feel. Discuss which are round, or have corners, or are long and thin, and which item is heavier or lighter than another. Introduce some mathematical names for shapes, such as: circle, square, rectangle, triangle, sphere, cube and cylinder.

Extensions

* Ask some of the children to pass two items to you at a time, instead of just one.

* Ask children to pass items to other practitioners or to each other, rather than always to the leader.

* Give clues instead of labels. For example: I need to brush my hair – could you pass me something that I could use, please? Could you please pass me something that I could use for my drink? Could you please pass something smooth and heavy to me now? I would like a cube and a sphere please.

Learning objectives linked to Early Learning Goals

(See pages 8–13 for abbreviations.)

* CL–LA: 9, 11
* CL–U: 1, 3, 6, 8
* PSED–MR: 5, 7
* PSED–MFB: 6
* EAD–EUMM: 12
* UW–W: 1, 2
* M–SSM: 6, 7, 8, 11

Contrasts

Equipment and resources

A large clear space with a safe ground or floor surface for movement. One or two practitioners to lead the game and possibly more practitioners to play the game with the children. Two percussion instruments that make very different sounds, such as bells and a drum or a triangle and a maraca.

Activity

✱ Invite the players to stand in spaces and listen carefully to the different sounds that the two instruments make. Decide together on an appropriate movement for each and practise them. For example: march to a drum beat and wriggle when bells are shaken, or tiptoe to a triangle's chimes and spin around when a maraca is played.

✱ Play the instruments firmly, making the contrasting sounds and swapping them frequently at random. Encourage the children to change their movement every time the sound changes.

Extensions

✱ Use three instruments instead of two. For example: jump when a drum plays, dance to a tune played on a kazoo and walk while a tambourine is shaken.

✱ Introduce freezing and balancing alongside other movements. For example: skip while the bells are played but balance on one leg when a triangle is struck and stay still until you hear the bells again, or stamp around while the maraca is shaken but freeze when you hear a loud drum beat and wait until you hear the maraca again before you move.

✱ Begin by sitting on the floor or ground and jump up to make the contrasting movements when instruments are played. Sit down again if all instruments stop suddenly and there is silence.

Learning objectives linked to Early Learning Goals

(See pages 8–13 for abbreviations.)
✱ CL–LA: 3
✱ CL–U: 8, 11
✱ PSED–MR: 5
✱ PD–MH: 6
✱ EAD–EUMM: 1, 5, 8, 9

© Debbie Chalmers and Brilliant Publications

Noisy stories

Equipment and resources

A large clear space. One practitioner to lead the activity and possibly more practitioners to support the children. A big book version of a story that includes a variety of sounds. Percussion instruments and other objects that can be used to create the different sounds.

Activity

* Invite the children to sit in a group from which they can all see the book clearly. Hand out one instrument or other object to each person. Name the instruments and objects in turn and explain the sound each will represent. Encourage the children to hold them up as you talk about them and to practise making the sounds. If the group is large enough, two or three people might make each sound.

* Read the story, pausing for each sound and encouraging those holding the appropriate instruments or objects to take their cues and use them. For example: It was raining hard (shake maracas). The horses galloped down the road (bang wooden blocks or coconut shells together). The clowns started to play their trumpets (use kazoos). The gardener tipped the stones out of the wheelbarrow (drop marbles onto a tray) and walked out to the street (tap out footsteps on a drum), to watch the circus procession go by through the puddles (shake some water in a tightly sealed bottle).

Extensions

* Use rhyme and poetry books with repetitive words and sounds and encourage children to make their sounds on cue to retain the rhythms.

* Give each child a different object and sound, so that they may concentrate, remember and participate individually. Ensure that a practitioner can support any child who is unable to confidently participate alone.

* Ask the children to stand up each time they make their sounds and then to immediately sit down again.

Learning objectives linked to Early Learning Goals

(See pages 8–13 for abbreviations.)
* CL–LA: 1, 7, 8, 9, 11
* CL–U: 5, 8
* PSED–SCSA: 2, 4
* EAD–EUMM: 4, 5, 11
* EAD–BI: 8
* L–R: 7, 10, 16
* UW–W: 2

© Debbie Chalmers and Brilliant Publications

Move in time

Equipment and resources
A large clear space with a safe ground or floor surface for movement. One practitioner to lead the game and more practitioners to support the children. CDs featuring pieces of music with different beats and tempos (songs, instrumentals, backing tracks and excerpts), such as: children's music, stage and screen musicals, popular music, dance tunes, classical, jazz, country and rock 'n' roll. A CD player.

Activity
*   Play different pieces of music, one after the other, and encourage the children to move in appropriate ways, following the speed and beat of the music that they can hear. Some tunes might suggest marching, others walking and others slow and swaying movements. Remind them of the need to move safely amongst others within the group.

*   Model a variety of movements for the children by joining in with the activity, but all practitioners should be aware that different sounds may suggest different moves to adults and to children and avoid expecting them to copy what they see.

*   Encourage children and adults to also clap, hum or sing along to any tunes that they know, if they wish to. Invite them to freeze, or sit down, or make an interesting shape, or perform a movement on the spot during the short silences between pieces of music.

Extensions
*   Play very contrasting pieces of music consecutively, encouraging children to move quickly, then slowly, then noisily, then quietly.

*   Suggest to the children that they may hear more than one timing in a tune and demonstrate for them how to walk or march at a steady pace, with one step for each beat (single time), or quickly, with two steps for each beat (double time), or slowly, with one step for each two beats (half time).

*   Provide opportunities for children to perform movements individually or within a pair or a small group, if they would like to, for the rest of the group to watch. Support all children as they learn how to be a good audience for each other.

Learning objectives linked to Early Learning Goals
(See pages 8–13 for abbreviations.)
*   CL–LA: 4, 9, 10, 11
*   PSED–MR: 5
*   PD–MH: 2, 6, 7
*   EAD–EUMM: 2, 3, 8, 13
*   EAD–BI: 2, 3, 7

Tidy up time!

Equipment and resources

A large clear space with a safe ground or floor surface for movement. One practitioner to lead the game and more practitioners to support the children. CDs featuring favourite songs that are likely to inspire speed, movement and co-operation. A CD player. Toys and equipment that need to be tidied away – at the end of a free play session or group activity.

Activity

* Explain to the children that tidying up is fun when everybody works together. Invite them to gather as a group in the centre of the play area and listen carefully.

* Ask each child individually, by name, to perform a specific task. For example: Vicky – please put the books that are on the carpet back onto the shelves. Divide larger tasks between small groups of children, giving them each specific jobs. For example: Greg – please collect up all the engines and trucks and put them into the train set boxes. Tess – please put the track pieces into the train set boxes. Andy – please put the tunnels, stations and engine sheds into the train set boxes. Remind them of how to move and carry different toys and equipment carefully and safely, asking for help if it is needed.

* Once all of the children have begun their allotted tasks, put on a favourite song and challenge them to complete their tidying up by the time the music ends. Practitioners should offer support to selected children as necessary to keep them on task and praise them all as they complete their objectives.

* Choose a song or medley of songs that is long enough to provide just enough time to complete the tasks comfortably. Also point out the time on the wall clock and explain where

the hands will be when the song ends, as some children may be less familiar with the song but beginning to recognise the passing of time in this way.

* Praise all of the children for completing the tasks they were given responsibility for.

Extensions

* Play the game outdoors, encouraging children to run around and collect up physical play equipment, move wheeled vehicles to where they may be parked and fit toys into their outdoor storage areas.

* Give a small group a collection of similar pieces that have been mixed up, such as a set of jigsaw puzzles or pens, pencils and crayons, and ask them to sort out the muddle. Suggest to each child that they collect the pieces for a different picture puzzle or a different type of pencil and put them away neatly.

* Explain a tidying task to a pair or small group of children and encourage them to choose how to carry it out together, considering how they tidy up their own toys or equipment at home.

Learning objectives linked to Early Learning Goals

(See pages 8–13 for abbreviations.)
* CL–LA: 5, 10
* CL–U: 1, 9, 11
* PSED–MR: 1, 4, 7
* PSED–SCSA: 2, 3, 4, 6, 7
* PSED–MFB: 6
* PD–MH: 3, 8
* PD–HSC: 4, 5
* EAD–EUMM: 2, 15
* M–SSM: 14

Explanation of the development of listening skills in children aged 4-5 years

This statement of age is only a rough guide, as all children are individuals and will acquire skills and develop abilities at different times and different rates.

Much will depend upon the experiences and stimulation that they receive from the environments and relationships provided by their homes and the early years settings and schools that they attend.

However, children are likely to acquire skills more or less in the following order, at the pace that is right for them.

● Participating in games to move when music plays or sounds are made and stop or change movement when the music or sounds stop.

● Sitting quietly and maintaining attention and concentration appropriately during a group activity.

● Waiting for a signal before carrying out an action, such as beginning to run when an adult shouts Go! or fetching a bag and a coat when a teacher says Home time.

● Following instructions involving more than one action.

● Identifying sounds heard without visual clues, such as emergency sirens, cars passing outside, thunder, dogs barking or babies crying.

● Listening to and considering others' ideas and using them to create more involved and satisfying play.

● Responding to others' speech while engaged in another activity.

● Knowing who is speaking without looking at them.

● Matching words that begin with the same phonetic sound.

● Recognising and repeating alliteration and rhyme.

● Beginning to understand and enjoy fantasy ideas, nonsense rhymes and jokes.

Do it to order

Equipment and resources

A large clear space. One practitioner to lead the activity and possibly more practitioners to support the children. One hat for each child and each adult. Six wooden or plastic blocks for each child and each adult (not interlocking). Two percussion instruments to make sounds as signals. Other clothing items, wellington boots, small-world toys.

Activity

* Invite the children to sit on the floor with their hats and blocks in front of them. Begin by giving a single instruction, such as: put on your hat, build a tower of three blocks or hold one block in each hand. Give children time to follow the instruction before carrying out the action yourself. Encourage them to look at you and at each other to check that everybody is performing the same action. Say Stop! and model replacing the hat and blocks on the floor and returning your hands to your lap. Give more single instructions, saying Stop! between each one.

* Repeat the game using two instructions together, such as: tap two blocks together, then hide them under the hat; turn the hat over, then put five blocks inside it; put the hat on your head, then balance a block on top of it. Use Stop! between each instruction, as before.

* Move on to sequences of three instructions, such as: build a tower of four blocks, then hold the other two blocks in one hand and pick up your hat with the other hand; swap two blocks with a friend, throw one gently into the air and try to catch it, then pass it carefully to a different friend; balance three blocks on one hand, then put them on your head and cover them up by putting your hat on top. Use Stop! between each sequence, encouraging the children to say it when they have carried out the instructions.

Extensions

* Invite children to take turns to make up instructions and demonstrate them for the group to copy. Ensure that they maintain concentration and listen carefully to each other.

* Use a sound made by a percussion instrument to signify Go! after speaking each sequence of instructions and ask children to wait to hear it before they move. Use a different sound to signify Stop! between each one.

* Add more clothing items, such as scarves and gloves, or more varied toys, such as small-world animals or vehicles, and develop more complicated instructions.

* Include wellington boots to pull on and off and add more movements for children to carry out while wearing them, such as stamping, jumping, hopping and balancing.

Learning objectives linked to Early Learning Goals

(See pages 8–13 for abbreviations.)

* CL–LA: 10, 11
* CL–U: 3, 7, 8, 9
* PSED–MR: 2, 7, 8
* PD–MH: 1, 8
* EAD–BI: 7
* M–SSM: 1, 13

Please join in

Equipment and resources

A large clear space with a safe ground or floor surface for movement. One practitioner to lead the game and more practitioners to support the children.

Activity

* Invite children to play a game in which manners are most important. Begin by standing in spaces. Explain that you will ask them to create movements, but that they should only obey if you remember to say please.

* Offer instructions such as: Please raise your arm. Please jump up and down. Turn around on the spot. Please clap your hands. Encourage the children to remind each other when they should not move because you forgot to say please (as in the game Simon Says).

* When the children are confident, introduce another rule for the game. After each instruction that the children obey, you should say thank you. If you remember, they should continue to make the movement until the next instruction, but, if you 'forget', they should stop again immediately.

Extensions

* Involve the children in interactions with each other, by giving instructions such as: Girls, please stand behind boys. If you are four, please hold hands with somebody who is five (or three). Please make circles of four people.

* Use two actions for each instruction, to be repeated alternately, such as: Please make three jumps, then tiptoe around in a circle.

* Invite all of the children to make a continuous movement, such as dancing, swaying or walking. Ask them to begin one at a time when they hear you say their names followed by please and to stop individually when they hear you say Thank you with their names. For example: Richard please. Fern please. Thank you Tara. Thank you William.

Learning objectives linked to Early Learning Goals

(See pages 8–13 for abbreviations.)

* CL–LA: 5, 10
* CL–U: 2, 7, 9
* PSED–MR: 1, 5
* PD–MH: 2, 3
* PD–HSC: 4
* EAD–EUMM: 1
* EAD–BI: 7
* M–N: 5
* M–SSM: 5, 9

Speaking and Listening Activities for the Early Years

Make a sound story

Equipment and resources

A large clear space. One practitioner to lead the activity and more practitioners to support the children. A selection of percussion instruments and other items that may be used to create sounds, such as: wooden blocks, marbles, tissue paper, metal spoons, rice in a tin and jigsaw puzzle pieces in a cardboard box.

Activity

* Invite the children to explore the instruments and other items and find out how many different sounds they can make. Encourage them to discuss the sound effects that they could create and the type of story that would need them.

* Support the children in making up a new story as a group, encouraging them all to contribute ideas and to decide on characters, setting, plot and sequence of events, adapting it to include as many sound effects as possible. They must work together to create all the sounds they need and to work out where they should occur within the story.

* Scribe the story and notes on its sounds for the children (and as a reminder for the practitioners supporting the storytellers), encouraging them to write and draw as much as they wish. Add the sound effects and tell the story, practising it several times until the children are confident. Arrange for them to perform the story with its sounds to any other children and to the adults in the setting.

Extensions

* Make available a box of instruments and objects to create interesting sound effects and encourage children to use them freely in their role-play.

* Ask children to name their favourite storybook or television characters and encourage them to create different sound effects or very short tunes for each character.

* Take a theme and challenge children to create a variety of relevant sounds. For example: suggest weather and support them in making sounds for rain, hail, snow, thunder, wind and sunshine.

Learning objectives linked to Early Learning Goals

(See pages 8–13 for abbreviations.)

* CL–LA: 1, 6
* CL–U: 11
* PSED–MR: 7, 9, 10, 11
* PSED–SCSA: 8
* EAD–EUMM: 4, 5, 11, 14, 15
* EAD–BI: 6, 8

Shake and guess

Equipment and resources

A large clear space. One practitioner to lead the activity and two or three more practitioners to play the game with the children. A percussion instrument that can be shaken, such as a maraca, a set of bells or a small tambourine.

Activity

* Invite the children and adults to sit in a circle. Practise passing the instrument around the circle, with each person taking it and passing it on with their hands behind their back. Then pass it around again, allowing each person to practise taking it, shaking it behind their back, then passing it on.

* Ask one practitioner to move away from the circle while the instrument is passed around again and to return suddenly. The players should immediately stop moving. After a short period of silence, the player presently holding the instrument behind his back should shake it gently and the adult should guess who has it and point to the person.

* Invite one or two children at a time to move away, then come back to guess and point to who is shaking the instrument. Ensure that it is a listening game, by reminding the players to keep their bodies very still and their hands hidden while shaking the instrument.

Extensions

* Sit in a line instead of a circle, with an adult at each end, and pass the instrument up and down the line behind the players' backs. It is surprisingly more difficult for the players to predict when the instrument will reach them when it moves back and forth in this way.

* Demonstrate three different instruments before the game starts. Swap them at random each time players move away and ask them to guess which instrument is being shaken as well as who is shaking it.

* Involve at least three or four practitioners in the game and give them each a small shaker to hide in their hands and shake at intervals. Invite all players to walk around each other at random and to freeze whenever they hear a shaker and point to the adult who is shaking it.

Learning objectives linked to Early Learning Goals

(See pages 8–13 for abbreviations.)

* CL–LA: 10, 11
* PSED–MR: 5, 7
* PSED–MFB: 5, 6, 9, 12
* EAD–EUMM: 4, 14, 15

Find the sound

Equipment and resources

A large clear space with a safe ground or floor surface for movement. Four or five practitioners. Noisy items that can be operated discreetly and will play for a short while, such as: musical toys, books that play sounds and tunes, toy vehicles with sirens, soft toy animals that make sounds and dolls that laugh or cry.

Activity

* Three practitioners should sit in spaces on the floor. The other practitioner(s) should sit with the group of children a short distance away. The adults should press or wind a toy in turn, to activate its sound, without it being visible to the children. Encourage the children to walk over to any sound that they hear and sit down beside it.

* At first, stop after each sound, praise the children who moved to the right place and invite them to guess and name what made the sound. Then show them the toy, encourage the other children to join the group and demonstrate the sound again.

* When most children are confident enough, gradually speed up the game by making another sound as soon as each one ends and encouraging them to sit down beside a sound until it stops, then jump up immediately and go to the new one.

* Note carefully which children confidently lead the game or listen and think independently, and which follow the group but may not be able to hear, understand or react at that level without support.

Extensions

* Instead of the whole group moving every time, ask each child or pair of children to play in turn, in order to check and develop confidence and understanding.

* Use the same sound, or two or three sounds in turn, operated by the practitioners in the three different places at random, so that children need to focus on the direction of the sound and not just learn and remember which sound is in which place. If identical toys are not available, use sounds such as: tapping on the floor, gently shaking some bells or rustling some paper.

* Play and stop each sound several times, asking children to move towards it but freeze every time it stops, until they finally reach it. For this, use sounds that are manually operated or can be paused and restarted easily.

Learning opportunities linked to Early Learning Goals

(See pages 8–13 for abbreviations.)
* CL–LA: 3, 9
* CL–U: 5, 8
* CL–S: 3, 6
* PSED–MR: 1, 2
* PSED–MFB: 9
* EAD–EUMM: 11, 14
* UW–W: 4

What's hiding?

Equipment and resources

A large clear space. One practitioner to lead the activity and possibly more practitioners to support the children. A selection of percussion instruments that make different and contrasting sounds. A large tray. A large cloth.

Activity

* Ask the children to sit in a circle or group, where they can all see the tray. Hold up each instrument in turn, name it and invite the children to listen to its sound as you play it, then place it on the tray. When all of the instruments have been named and demonstrated, cover them with the cloth.

* Play one instrument at a time, in a random order, hidden under the cloth, and invite the children to guess which one it is. If you find that a few children always guess quickly while others do not offer any ideas, ask each child by name to take a turn at guessing and enlist the support of other practitioners in helping the quicker children to wait and listen to others, rather than calling out.

Extensions

* Introduce instruments that can make two or more different sounds, such as a tambourine which may be tapped or shaken, and support children in understanding that either sound may lead to the same answer.

* Play one instrument followed by another and ask children whether they can name them both. Build up to longer sequences, challenging some children to name four or more different instruments in the order they heard them.

* Use other items, instead of instruments, to create everyday sounds for the children to identify, such as: the jangling of a bunch of keys, the rustling of a comic or newspaper, the cutting of paper with scissors and the rolling of marbles.

Learning opportunities linked to Early Learning Goals

(See pages 8–13 for abbreviations.)
* CL–LA: 3, 6, 9, 11
* CL–U: 8, 11
* CL–S: 3, 5, 16
* PSED–MR: 1, 10
* PSED–MFB: 9, 10
* EAD–EUMM: 11, 14

Put us together

Equipment and resources

A large clear space. One practitioner to lead the activity and more practitioners to support the children. A selection of objects or pictures of objects that form recognised pairs, such as: a brush and a comb, a knife and a fork, a shoe and a sock, a pencil and paper, a scarf and gloves.

Activity

* Invite the children and adults to sit in a circle and place the objects or pictures in the centre. Point to each in turn and name it. Encourage the group to discuss the pairs of objects that go together.

* Hold up one object or picture and ask a practitioner first: What do I need to go with this (shoe)? The practitioner should pick up the matching item and offer it to you, so that you may take it and say: Yes, a (sock). Ask each person in turn, holding up a different object or picture each time.

* Once children are confident, ask the questions, such as: What do I need to go with a (pencil)? without touching the named item and ask them to offer you the appropriate item for the pair as before, telling you its name if they can.

Extensions

* Introduce more subtle differences between the pairs of objects or pictures. For example, match: the red brick and the yellow brick, the big teddy and the little teddy or the old book and the new book. Move onto models or pictures that belong to the same group but can look quite different, such as: dogs, fish, cakes, vegetables and cars. Challenge children to put the groups together and learn some of the names of the items.

* Discuss materials and textures and use a variety of toys, so that you may ask for: something else made of hard wood or shiny metal or soft fabric or smooth plastic, something else that is heavy or light or something else that feels rough or smooth.

* Invite preferences using pictures or photographs of activities and places. Hold up a picture of a place as you ask: What do you like to do indoors at nursery? or outside at nursery? or at home? or in your bedroom? or in your garden? or at the park? Children should point to a picture of an activity, such as: drawing, running, reading, sand play or using a swing, and name or talk about it if they can.

Learning opportunities linked to Early Learning Goals

(See pages 8–13 for abbreviations.)

* CL–LA: 11
* CL–U: 1, 4, 5, 6, 8, 11
* CL–S: 5, 15, 16
* PSED–MR: 5, 10
* PSED–SCSA: 1, 2, 8
* PSED–MFB: 9
* EAD–EUMM: 12
* UW–W: 2, 4, 5

Sequence of moves

Equipment and resources

A large clear space with a safe ground or floor surface for movement. One practitioner to lead the activity and more practitioners to support the children and ensure their safety. Three pieces of large play equipment, such as: a tunnel, a trampette and a wooden climbing block or a tyre, a plank and a cardboard box, together with appropriate safety surfaces or mats.

Activity

* Set out the pieces of equipment separately, using any required safety surfaces or mats and allowing enough room between them for children to safely move around. Invite the children to explore the items and demonstrate the first movements you will ask them to make. Talk with the children about the ways in which exercise contributes to good health.

* Speak each child's name in turn and give them each a sequence of three moves to follow. For example: Crawl through the tunnel, then jump five times on the trampette, then stand and balance on the block. Jump into the tyre and out again, then walk along the plank, then sit inside the box.

* Support children as they try to remember and carry out each movement. Encourage them to remember and stick to the order of the sequence if possible, asking for reminders if they feel that they need them. Then invite them to tell the group what they did.

* Discuss safety measures and possible risks and challenges throughout the activity, encouraging children to recognise and manage these for themselves and each other.

Extensions

* Add smaller items of physical play equipment, such as hoops, balls, beanbags and skipping ropes, to enhance the movements. For example, ask children to: throw a beanbag into the hoop; roll a ball along the plank; skip around the tyre.

* Introduce sequences of instructions into daily routines within the setting and encourage children to listen and concentrate in order to follow them. For example: go to wash your hands, then sit down for lunch, then pour your drink from the jug. Continue to discuss healthy eating and hygiene practices.

* Model thinking sequences by speaking aloud when engaged in play activities. Say, for example: I'm going to find the tray of pencils, draw a picture and write my name on it. I'll finish building my model, I'll take a photo of it, then I'll tidy away the rest of the bricks.

Learning opportunities linked to Early Learning Goalss

(See pages 8–13 for abbreviations.)

* CL–U: 3, 5, 7, 9
* CL–S: 9, 13, 17
* PSED–MR: 7
* PSED–SCSA: 7, 9
* PSED–MFB: 9, 11
* PD–MH: 1, 2, 4
* PD–HSC: 3, 4
* M–SSM: 4

Who's talking?

Equipment and resources

A large clear space. Three practitioners, whose voices are very familiar to the children, to lead the activity and one or two more practitioners to support the children. A screen or partition, or an adjoining room with an open door. A story or poetry book or an agreed list of well-known rhymes.

Activity

* Invite the children to sit in a group with one or two adults while three adults go to stand behind the screen, partition or door, close to the group but not visible to them. Talk with the children about people having different voices, even when they speak the same words, and how we can recognise our families and friends and other familiar people because we are used to the sounds of their voices and the ways in which they speak.

* The practitioners should take turns to read from the book or speak rhymes, while the children try to guess who is speaking. As soon as a child calls out the correct name, the adult should stop speaking and step out to wave to the group, then hide again as a different adult begins to speak.

* The game can continue until each adult has spoken and been guessed several times. Make it more difficult by sometimes having the same adult speak again immediately once they have hidden.

Extensions

* Ask two practitioners to speak a rhyme together, either in unison or taking character parts or alternate lines, and challenge the children to guess them both.

* Ask a practitioner to stop just before the last line of a rhyme, or at significant words within it, and encourage the children to call out the missing words.

* Invite any children who feel confident enough to go behind the screen, partition or door with the adults and take turns to speak rhymes while the group guesses who is speaking. Support the children in listening carefully to work out who is there, rather than looking around the group to see who is missing!

Learning opportunities linked to Early Learning Goals

(See pages 8–13 for abbreviations.)
* CL–LA: 2, 9, 11
* PSED–MFB: 9, 11, 13
* L–R: 2, 10
* UW–PC: 5, 10

Sound mixing

Equipment and resources

A large clear space. One practitioner to lead the activity and possibly more practitioners to support the children. One percussion instrument for each child and adult that can be tapped and shaken, such as a tambourine, drum, maraca or set of handbells.

Activity

* Demonstrate the sounds that the instrument can make and how to hold and use it safely. Encourage the children to explore the different sounds that they can make with the instrument using various techniques, but introduce a few rules to avoid accidents and damage, as children of this age can be very inventive! For example: a tambourine may be shaken, tapped against the hand or placed on the floor and tapped with fingers or a beater: it should not be placed on the head and allowed to fall to the floor, banged too hard, clashed against another instrument or thrown.

* Invite the children to copy your sounds. Begin with simple rhythms, such as three shakes or four taps, and gradually move on to sequences, such as two hand taps, three beats, one long shake. Ask them to replace their instruments on the floor in front of them after making each set of sounds, in order to listen to the next sequence without noise distractions.

Extensions

* Introduce a simple repetitive rhythmic beat and challenge the children to maintain it for as long as they can, supported by adults playing it with them.

* Try using two different instruments, encouraging children to use one and then the other and then to combine them in sequences, such as: two drum beats, two maraca shakes.

* Invite children to take turns to create a sequence or rhythm for the group to copy.

Learning opportunities linked to Early Learning Goals

(See pages 8–13 for abbreviations.)

* CL–LA: 3, 9, 11
* CL–U: 6, 8, 9
* PSED–MFB: 9, 13
* PD–MH: 4, 8
* PD–HSC: 5
* EAD–EUMM: 1, 4, 10, 11, 14, 15
* EAD–BI: 3

Speaking and Listening Activities for the Early Years

Up and down

Equipment and resources

A large clear space. One practitioner to lead the activity and possibly more practitioners to support the children. A piano or keyboard or similar instrument. (A xylophone or glockenspiel can work equally well. A small children's instrument may be used if it can play at least one octave of notes clearly.)

Activity

* Gather the children and adults to sit together as a group close to the instrument. Play one or more octaves of notes several times and ask the children to listen carefully to hear the tune going up and down, up and down. Repeat the scales, playing loudly and then softly, and ask the children if they can hear the difference. Finally, play them again with a staccato beat and then smoothly, asking the children to listen for the bumpy sounds and the smooth sounds.

* Play a game in which you play octaves of notes and the children call out what they hear for each one in turn, such as: going up, bumpy, loud, going down, smooth, soft.

* Suggest that they make up movements or actions for each type of sound to carry out as well as naming them. They might choose to stretch up and stand on tiptoes, crouch down and curl up, stamp their feet, put a finger to their lips, hop and sway. Practitioners could offer suggestions or model some movements at first if they are not sure.

Extensions

* Invite the children to make their movements as soon as they hear the notes, but to freeze as soon as the notes stop and change their movements appropriately immediately they hear the next ones.

* Play only three to six notes, instead of the full octave, and challenge children to listen first and then make their movements for the correct number of counts after the notes end. For example: stretching up for six counts, crouching down for three counts, making five stamps or four sways.

* Encourage the group to discuss, create and agree on a sequence of movements, using their ideas in a creative order, such as: stamping, hopping, stretching up, swaying, holding a finger to lips, crouching down. Invite them to perform their sequence while you play the notes for them in the correct ways to act as a reminder.

Learning opportunities linked to Early Learning Goals

(See pages 8–13 for abbreviations.)
* CL–LA: 9, 10
* CL–U: 5, 8, 11
* CL–S: 17
* PSED–MR: 5, 8
* PSED–SCSA: 8
* PD–MH: 6
* EAD–EUMM: 1, 8, 9
* M–N: 5, 7

Explanation of the development of speaking skills in children aged 2-3 years

This statement of age is only a rough guide, as all children are individuals and will acquire skills and develop abilities at different times and different rates.

Much will depend upon the experiences and stimulation that they receive before the age of two years and the environments and relationships provided by their homes and the early years settings that they attend.

However, children are likely to acquire skills more or less in the following order, at the pace that is right for them.

● Naming familiar people in photographs.

● Naming objects and characters in pictures and storybooks.

● Making choices by expressing yes or no in any spoken or signed language.

● Linking two words together for meaning, such as more drink.

● Verbalising personal needs, such as being tired, hungry, thirsty, sad, cross or happy, using appropriate words or phrases.

● Stringing words together to try to create simple phrases and sentences, such as Go bed teddy blanket.

● Giving relevant answers when spoken to by an adult or a child.

● Using verbs and adjectives as well as nouns.

● Describing their own activities using sequences of photographs and adult support.

● Beginning to join in with parts of favourite rhymes, songs and stories.

● Asking adults for help, support or reassurance when needed.

● Engaging in conversation with an adult or a child to explain specific play ideas or feelings.

● Asking questions of an adult or a child, such as Can I play? May I have a turn? Why are you sad?

● Participating in general conversations and chats with adults and children, one-to-one and in small groups.

● Developing greater clarity and fluency in speech, although some infantilisms may persist and some sounds may be substituted for others.

May I have it please?

Equipment and resources

A large clear space. One practitioner for each two or three children, all of whom understand how to model the correct speech throughout the activity. Four popular toys, such as a teddy, a car, a book and a ball.

Activity

* Invite the children and practitioners to sit in a circle or a group. Hold the toys on your lap. Ask the practitioners, in turn, which toys they would like. The practitioners should reply: I would like the (teddy) please. (Ensure that the name of the toy and the word please appear last in the sentence, as that is the part that a very young child will hear and remember.) Pass the named toys to the practitioners, one by one, until all of the toys have been given out.

* Ask all children in turn, by name, which toys they would like. When they reply, the practitioner or child holding the appropriate toy should pass it. (Some children may need support to pass the toy to another child when they are holding it.)

* Encourage all children to attempt to say the sentence: I would like the (toy) please, but accept that some may only be able to manage one or two words. Praise all attempts that include the name of the toy and/or the word please, and also praise the children for listening to each other, waiting for their turns and passing and holding the toys gently.

* When each child has had one or more turns, end the game by asking practitioners again, until all of the toys are held by adults.

Extensions

* Model offering toys to each other, saying: Would you like the (ball)? and replying with: Yes please or No thank you. Encourage children to do this with practitioners and then with each other. They may be able to move on to dialogues such as: Would you like the teddy? No thank you, I'd like the car.

* Have several of each of the toys available. Hold up a toy and ask the group: Who would like the (book)? Encourage children to reply with the whole sentence: I would like the (book) please. Pass the appropriate toys to all children who accurately say as much as they are able to.

* After modelling the question and possible responses with practitioners, ask children in turn: What would you like to play with? Encourage children to point or walk to an appropriate toy box, piece of equipment or area of the room and reply: I would like to play with (the playdough) please.

Learning objectives linked to Early Learning Goals

(See pages 8–13 for abbreviations.)

* CL–LA: 5
* CL–U: 4, 8
* CL–S: 1, 5, 8, 13, 14, 21
* PSED–SCSA: 1, 3, 8
* PSED–MFB: 5, 9
* PD–MH: 8

Yes or no?

Equipment and resources

A large clear space. One practitioner to lead the activity and two or three more practitioners to participate, demonstrate and support the children. A set of picture cards (photographs or drawings) depicting the items that you wish to offer to the children within the setting, such as foods and drinks for snacktime, or mark-making tools and colours in the craft area, or outdoor toys in the garden.

Activity

* Demonstrate non-verbal signs for Yes and No, saying the words clearly as you sign them. Offer the picture cards to a practitioner first, one by one. The adult should reply with No to several cards until replying Yes to one and receiving the item. Offer cards to each child and adult in turn, encouraging children to speak or sign Yes or No, or to use both words and signs if possible, and stopping when a Yes response is received.

* Another practitioner should give each child what they have asked for immediately, while the game continues, to ensure that they associate the communication with the gratification.

* Non-verbal, pre-verbal, very young and under confident children can benefit from this activity, as can those with disabilities or special needs and those speaking English as an additional language. It can also show the other children how to help and support those who are still learning to communicate and those with differing needs. Continue to use this method of offering choices across the setting, to ensure that learning to communicate is meaningful and useful and children will want to work at it in order to receive appropriate rewards.

Extensions

* Add signs for please and thank you with appropriate symbolic illustrations on picture cards. Encourage children to put the two pairs of signs together to form Yes please and No thank you and to attempt to speak the words as they sign them. Ensure that children who do not yet use much speech are exposed to adults and their older and more verbally confident peers, to encourage them to want to join in with the conversations around them.

* Learn signs to accompany popular songs, rhymes and stories and perform them as you sing or read aloud at group times. Encourage all children to join in and attempt to copy both words and signs.

* If your setting includes children with disabilities, who cannot learn to speak fluently, invite family members or carers to come in to teach more signs or other communication methods to both adults and children.

Learning opportunities linked to Early Learning Goals

(See pages 8–13 for abbreviations.)
* CL–LA: 2, 4, 6, 9
* CL–U: 4, 5
* CL–S: 1, 6, 14
* PSED–SCSA: 1, 2
* PSED–MFB: 1, 13
* UW–PC: 1

Hello and goodbye

Equipment and resources

A large clear space with a safe ground or floor surface. One practitioner to lead the activity and more practitioners to support the children and ensure their safety. Play equipment that allows children to move closer and then further away, such as a swing, a seesaw or a rocking chair, or to hide and pop out then hide again, such as a tent, a playhouse or a blanket.

Activity

* Invite children to sit on the moving equipment or inside or under the hiding place. Gently begin the back and forth or in and out movement.

* Each time a child comes close to you, express pleasure by smiling and clapping your hands and say Hello! When a child moves away or hides, wave and say Goodbye! Use these greetings in each child's first language as well as in the language spoken in the setting.

* Involve other practitioners, so that each child may experience this game on a one-to-one basis with an adult.

* Encourage the children to speak the words and perform the actions themselves too. Some may be encouraged to describe where they are, saying: Under the blanket! or In the tent!

Extensions

* Add the children's names after Hello and Goodbye and encourage them to reply using the adults' names.

* Substitute other phrases, to extend the children's vocabularies and allow them to understand that greetings may be given in many different ways, but the meaning is generally the same. For example: Nice to see you. I'm glad you're here. See you soon. Come back later. Include some jokes for children who are ready to enjoy them, such as: Why have you come back again? Are you still here? Don't get lost! I think you've disappeared!

* Encourage children to guess which of their friends are hiding and to call for them by name and then greet them. For example: Come back Jemima! Hello. She's come back! Where's Sean? Hello. He's here now! Support children in learning to call for friends and greet them in their first languages. Children can easily absorb several different ways of saying Hello and Goodbye and match them to the speakers of each language.

Learning opportunities linked to Early Learning Goals

(See pages 8–13 for abbreviations.)
* CL–LA: 6
* CL–U: 4, 5, 7
* CL–S: 5, 6, 8, 16
* PSED–MR: 1, 7
* PSED–MFB: 3, 12
* EAD–BI: 1, 5
* UW–PC: 3
* M–SSM: 9

© Debbie Chalmers and Brilliant Publications

Is it my turn now?

Equipment and resources

A suitable play area within the setting, indoors or outdoors. Two practitioners. A piece of popular play equipment that requires children to take turns, such as a xylophone or a slide, or two or three popular toys that must be shared, such as buckets in the sand tray or tricycles.

Activity

* One practitioner should model polite speech that expresses the wish to use the play equipment or toys. For example: May I be next? Could I share? The other practitioner should respond by saying: Yes you can and indicating the equipment or passing over a toy. They may elaborate further with phrases such as: Is it my turn now? May I have this one? It can be your turn after mine. You can share with me.

* Invite the children to form a line and follow each other to the play equipment or toys. Support all of the children as they each attempt to ask for a turn or to share and try to respond positively to each other. Allow each child a little time to play before encouraging the next child to ask for a turn. The children may learn to ask for their turns quite easily, but need more support to ensure that they give up the toys to others when requested.

Extensions

* Make the phrases longer by adding the good manners and social conventions that are usually expected within our culture, such as: Please may I be next? Could I share please? Is it my turn? Thank you.

* Encourage the children to remember and use the phrases independently whenever they want to play with others and support them all in giving positive responses, sharing and taking turns.

* Support and encourage those children who are ready to reach out to others and invite them to play, by suggesting phrases that they might use, such as: You can play too. Join in with me. You do it next.

Learning opportunities linked to Early Learning Goals

(See pages 8–13 for abbreviations.)

* CL–LA: 6
* CL–U: 1, 2, 4, 11
* CL–S: 2, 7, 21
* PSED–MR: 3, 6, 10
* PSED–SCSA: 2, 7, 8
* PSED–MFB: 3, 5, 9, 12, 13

Tell us what yo[u]

Equipment and resources

A safe clean floor surface indoors or a rug or blanket outside. One practitioner to lead the activity and possibly more practitioners to support and encourage the children. Photographs of a recent trip, visit or outing, a visitor to the setting, a special project undertaken or a special exploration of the outdoor area – to create a shared and relevant topic for discussion. A suitable plain wall or a display board if possible.

Activity

* Display the photos clearly and in a logical sequence by attaching them to a wall or display board or spreading them across the floor or rug. Point to the photos in turn and talk through what happened on that day, encouraging children to offer ideas, memories and explanations throughout. Encourage them to recognise signs and remember what they said, such as: 'No dogs' at the playground, the country code and maps in the woods, the name of a farm, or the 'Police' sign on the side of a car.

* Ask open questions, such as: Which animals did you like best at the farm? Was there anything you didn't like at the park? How did you feel when it was time to go back to nursery?

* Extend children's statements by saying, for example: So you liked all the baby animals, Eleanor, but you liked the little piglets and the little lambs best? We loved running on the grass in the park, but we didn't like the stinging nettles by the wall, did we? Especially when one touched Madeleine's leg! I think you were a bit sad to have to leave the woods, John, but quite pleased to go back to nursery to have a drink, because we all got so thirsty. So you remember that the police officer showed us his uniform and his radio and we saw the blue flashing lights on his car.

Extensions

* Mix up the phot[os] them in a pile to [ ] Challenge the chil[d] right order and des[cribe] events.

* Give one photo to eac[h child] and invite them in turn to tell the group one thing about the picture, such as: We wore our coats and our boots. We pretended to have a house under the slide. It was dark underneath the tall trees. We put the bandages from the doctor on our teddies and she showed us how to do it.

* Encourage the children to draw their own pictures and describe them. Scribe for them as they tell you about each mark they have made. Use your writing to remind yourself as you support them in talking about their pictures to the group.

Learning opportunities linked to Early Learning Goals

(See pages 8–13 for abbreviations.)
* CL–LA: 6, 11
* CL–U: 1, 4, 11
* CL–S: 2, 3, 9, 13, 14, 15, 18, 19, 20
* PSED–MR: 8, 9
* L–W: 1
* UW–PC: 1, 6, 7, 8
* UW–W: 5
* M–SSM: 13, 14

Take your turn

…pment and resources

…arge clear space. One practitioner to lead the activity and one or more practitioners to participate and support the children. A toy microphone or a soft toy or a small item that is satisfying to hold, such as a beanbag, a pine cone or a smooth stick.

Activity

✳ Invite the children and adults to sit in a circle. Begin by holding the item and explaining the rules of the activity. For example: Each person may speak into the microphone when they have it, or Each person may talk to teddy while he sits on their lap or Each person may tell us while they are holding the beanbag. Make it clear that everybody else should be listening until it is their turn to speak and then everybody will listen to them.

✳ Introduce a simple theme, such as how you are going to travel home from the setting today or whether you have any pets at home. Model a short, clear speech while holding the item, such as: I will go home from nursery on the bus. I don't have any pets but my granny has two cats. Then pass the item to the child beside you.

✳ Each child and adult may speak in turn, while everybody listens, then pass the item on. Support all children in remembering to speak only when they are holding the item. It can be passed around the circle as many times as desired. A child may choose not to speak at first, but simply to pass the item on. However, when the item is passed around the circle for the second or third time, many more children may feel confident enough to say something. Some children may only be able to say a word or two, such as: in car or dog. Others may be keen to offer more elaborate ideas, such as: I rode on my scooter to the school gate, then I walked across the road and I parked my scooter outside the preschool. My fish are orange and their names are Tangerine and Satsuma. At the end of the activity, praise all of the children for the relevant and interesting contributions that they made.

Extensions

✳ Use this activity on a Monday (or the first day each child attends your setting) to encourage the children to share descriptions of their weekends. However, if your setting offers sessional places and not all children attend every day, repeat it on other days of the week to ensure that all children have the opportunity to participate, in small or larger groups.

✳ Invite children to prepare introductory speeches to describe themselves and deliver them in turn while holding the item. For example: I'm Chloe and I'm three and I live in Cambridge. Support any children who are not ready to speak alone by allowing them to deliver their speeches to an adult or more confident child who will repeat them to the group.

✳ Choose a favourite nursery rhyme that all of the children know and play a game in which each person in turn takes the item, speaks the next one word of the rhyme and immediately passes it on. The item may move around the circle very rapidly, which encourages children to take cues and increase their speed and fluency. (As a guide: reciting Humpty Dumpty will cause the item to move around a circle of six people just over four times and a circle of twelve people just over two times.) It is surprisingly difficult to stop speaking after only one word in this situation, for adults as well as children, and so this game can cause much amusement.

Learning opportunities linked to Early Learning Goals

(See pages 8–13 for abbreviations.)

✳ CL–LA: 6, 9, 11
✳ PSED–SCSA: 6, 7, 8, 9
✳ CL–U: 5, 8, 11
✳ PSED–MFB: 2, 3, 7, 9, 10
✳ CL–S: 1, 2, 9, 12, 13, 14, 15, 18, 19
✳ L–R: 2, 7
✳ UW–PC: 2, 5, 6, 7, 8, 9

Choose your favourites

Equipment and resources

A place for each child to sit, either on a chair at a table or on the floor around a cloth. One practitioner to lead the activity and one or more practitioners to support the children and ensure their safety. Plates of different raw fruits and vegetables, chopped into small pieces or slices. (If any are hard to recognise in small pieces, such as pineapple, dragon fruit or carrot, also show the children a whole one or a picture or photograph of one.)

Activity

* Point to each fruit and vegetable in turn and name it for the children. Model saying: Carrot please or Strawberry please and taking one piece of the named food from a plate to eat. Encourage each child in turn, by name, to do the same, taking turns until all the food is gone or all children and adults have had enough to eat. Practitioners should show children how to choose a variety of pieces and encourage them to try new foods, by asking for different and unusual pieces at their turns, but ensure that there are plenty of pieces of the most popular foods that children will want to go on asking for, as this is first and foremost a speaking activity, although it can also serve as a healthy eating exercise.

* Support any children who only point to what they want by saying the words for them: Apple please? or asking them a question: Would you like this piece of pear? and encouraging them to repeat the names, or at least to say Yes or No. As children become more confident, encourage them all to say thank you as they take their pieces of food. If the adults model this from the beginning, some will do it naturally, as they have learned it at home, and others will quickly copy them.

Extensions

* Invite children to choose and ask for two different pieces of food at a time. For example: Melon and mango please or Sweetcorn and broccoli please.

* Repeat the activity, encouraging the children to link more words together and speak in polite sentences, such as: Please may I have banana?, I would like some mushroom please. Remind them again about saying thank you when they receive what they have asked for.

* Invite children in turn to look at all of the fruits and vegetables on the plates and tell the group about their preferences. For example: I like apples, grapes and carrots best and I do like raspberries and cucumber, but I don't like pineapple or cauliflower very much. Only a few children of this age are likely to manage to create an organised speech of this length, but, if the adults model speeches in this way, they will understand and gradually contribute more thoughts and opinions of their own.

Learning opportunities linked to Early Learning Goals

(See pages 8–13 for abbreviations.)
* CL–LA: 5, 6
* CL–U: 1, 4, 5, 11
* CL–S: 1, 5, 6, 13, 15, 16, 18
* PSED–MR: 8, 10
* PSED–SCSA: 1, 2, 8
* PSED–MFB: 1, 9, 10, 13
* UW–PC: 5
* UW–W: 5

© Debbie Chalmers and Brilliant Publications

I need to go

Equipment and resources

A large clear space. One practitioner to lead the activity and more practitioners to support the children. Small-world people with rooms and furniture. (This could be a dolls' house if playing with a small enough group, or separate paper 'floors' with furniture made from blocks or construction kits and any collection of play people figures available in the setting.)

Activity

*   Pick up a person and speak for it, saying: I need to go to sleep. Then place the person on a bed in a bedroom. Take another person and speak for it: I need to go to the toilet. Place the person in the bathroom. Take a third person and speak for it: I need to have a drink. Sit the person on a chair at a table in the kitchen or dining room. When the children have watched, listened and absorbed this, take all of the people back.

*   Give one person to each child and encourage them all to speak for their people, saying where they need to go and putting them in appropriate places. Allow them to move their people as many times as they wish. Adults may support children who seem unsure by suggesting that their people are tired or hungry or have dirty hands to wash and encouraging them to place the figures appropriately.

Extensions

*   When the children can confidently state basic needs, introduce choices and preferences, such as: I'd like to go upstairs. I'd like to go outside. I'd like to cook in the kitchen. Use the small-world figures and move them around as before.

*   Give a small group of children a family of small-world people and ask them to listen carefully while you tell them about each person. For example: The baby needs to go to sleep. The girl needs to have her lunch. The boy wants to play in the garden. The grandad would like to watch television. Deliberately omit to state what the mother and father figures would like to do and ask the children what they think they need to do. Encourage them to think about who might need help and supervision within the family and how to meet several needs at once. For example: Mummy puts the baby to bed and then gives the girl her lunch, while Daddy watches the boy playing in the garden because he needs to cut the grass too. Grandad can watch television by himself.

*   Encourage the children to use these phrases in the role-play area, when they are pretending to be a family in their home, speaking in character for themselves or for dolls or puppets.

Learning opportunities linked to Early Learning Goals

(See pages 8–13 for abbreviations.)

*   CL–LA: 6
*   CL–U: 2, 5, 11
*   CL–S: 2, 4, 17, 18, 19
*   PSED–MR: 3, 7, 9
*   PSED–SCSA: 2, 6
*   PSED–MFB: 4, 5, 9
*   PD–MH: 8
*   PD–HSC: 3
*   EAD–BI: 1, 4, 5, 6, 7
*   UW–PC: 3, 7
*   UW–W: 1, 3

Who cares for you?

Equipment and resources

A large clear space. One practitioner to lead the activity and possibly more practitioners to support the children. Photographs of at least one or two primary carers for each child (requested from home or taken at the setting at arrival time). Photographs of all practitioners.

Activity

* Sit comfortably with a small group of children and display the photographs in front of you. Encourage the children to point to or pick up the pictures of their own parents or carers and name them. (Ensure that you have duplicate pictures if you are including siblings or twins within the group, so that each may respond independently.) Support children in saying the names if they do not speak, ensuring correct pronunciation of any names from other languages and cultures and any nicknames or pet names used by the families.

* Encourage the children to point to and name the practitioners, especially each child's key person. Help them gradually to understand that different children use the same titles to mean different people, but that we can avoid confusion by speaking of them as: Ian's Daddy, Michelle's Mummy, Leon's Nana, George's Grandma, Kim's Grandad, José's Grandpa. They will also learn that all of the children in a class or setting share the same caring adults and simply use their names.

Extensions

* Spread out all of the photos and encourage the children to collect those of their own parents and carers and make their own family piles, which they then hold up and name for the group.

* Turn all the family and carer photos face down. Turn them over one at a time and encourage the children to say who each one belongs to and give it to the right child. Suggest to them that they stay quiet when they see their own pictures, to give the other children a chance to guess.

* Hold up the photos of the practitioners one by one and encourage the children to call out their names and wave to them if they can see them in the room.

Learning opportunities linked to Early Learning Goals

(See pages 8–13 for abbreviations.)
* CL–LA: 6
* CL–U: 11
* CL–S: 3, 14
* PSED–MR: 5, 8, 9, 10
* PSED–SCSA: 6, 9
* UW–PC: 1, 2, 5, 6, 10

© Debbie Chalmers and Brilliant Publications

All join in

Equipment and resources

A large clear space. Six practitioners. Four different activities suitable for group play, such as: a floor puzzle, a construction kit, a small-world farmyard and some mark making equipment.

Activity

* Four practitioners should sit in separate spaces and each should set out one activity attractively. Two practitioners should gather the children into a group and explain that they may choose where to play and ask to join in. One practitioner may demonstrate if necessary, then invite children to take turns to walk to their chosen areas.

* As each child approaches an activity, the adult there should welcome the child with an appropriate greeting, such as: Would you like to play?

* The child should be encouraged to say: Could I play too? Can I join in? May I play with you? or something similar. One adult may need to accompany and support some children while the other remains with the rest of the group.

* When children try to offer relevant speeches, they should be welcomed warmly and involved in the play activities they have chosen.

* Introduce this activity indoors at first, where children will be more easily able to see all of the activities on offer and hear what is being said. Once they are more confident, try it outside too; the idea will be the same, but children may need to move further from the group and speak more loudly.

Extensions

* After the children have played for a short time, suggest that they each choose a different play activity to move to and repeat the speeches, gradually decreasing adult support if possible.

* Divide the children into four groups and give each group a few toys. After they have played a little, ask the first group to walk over to the second group, who should ask them: Would you like to play? while they ask: Could we play with you? (Ensure that the answer is yes on both sides!) After they have played together for a minute or two, ask the second group to repeat this by moving over to the third group, then the third group with the fourth group. The fourth group can then move back to the first group, so every group has moved to join another and also received another group to play.

* Form a circle with half of the practitioners and children and play a short ring game. The other half of the group should then ask: Please may we join in? Encourage the children to drop hands and allow others into the circle, then re-form the (larger) ring and play again. Repeat the exercise with the other half of the group beginning the game.

Learning opportunities linked to Early Learning Goals

(See pages 8–13 for abbreviations.)
* CL–U: 4, 8
* CL–S: 2, 4, 7, 13, 14
* PSED–MR: 1, 2, 3, 6, 8
* PSED–SCSA: 2, 7, 8
* PSED–MFB: 3, 5, 6, 9, 11
* PD–MH: 2, 8
* EAD–EUMM: 6
* EAD–BI: 7

What if?

Equipment and resources

A large clear space. One practitioner to lead the activity and possibly more practitioners to support the children. Pictures or photographs of children carrying out routines and procedures within the setting, such as: washing hands, sitting at a table, lining up by a door and putting on coats. A plain wall or display board.

Activity

* Invite a group of children, whose speech is fairly well developed, to play the What If? game. Explain that you would like them to tell you what you need to do at different times, because you keep forgetting. Ask questions such as: What if it was lunchtime?

* Encourage the group to discuss the different tasks and put them into a correctly ordered sequence. For example: the children might say that you should go to the toilet, then wash your hands and then sit at the table.

* Support them at first by displaying the pictures or photos on a wall or board as visual clues and allowing them to move them around to create a sequence of tasks in a sensible order. Play the game on different occasions, gradually decreasing the dependence upon the pictures, and eventually removing them altogether.

* Include the routines of your setting, such as: What if we had just arrived here in the morning? What if it was time to go home? What if we wanted to play outside but it was very cold/very hot? Also include health and safety procedures, such as: What if we were going to make the snacks? What if we heard the fire alarm? What if we dropped the box of marbles and they rolled out all over the floor?

Extensions

* Discuss possible situations that might occur during free play periods and encourage children to use the game to help them to think of solutions to problems and compromises to solve conflicts. For example: What if four children wanted to play with two bikes? What if all the green paint was used up? What if some friends fell over and bumped their knees?

* Talk about the importance of caring for toys and equipment and what would happen if we were careless or destructive. Use dramatic and even silly examples to capture the attention of all the children, such as: What if we left all the pens outside in the grass with no lids on? What if we threw all the play people and animals all over the floor and then stepped on them? What if we dropped the teddies into the water tray?

* Enter the realms of fantasy and encourage imagination. For example: What if the nursery disappeared in the night? What if a monkey came to live in the garden? What if the park turned into the seaside? What if we could fly? Reassure any nervous children that these things will not really happen, but that they are fun to think about, like stories.

Learning opportunities linked to Early Learning Goals

(See pages 8–13 for abbreviations.)
* CL–LA: 6, 11
* CL–U: 4, 5, 9, 10, 11
* CL–S: 9, 14, 15, 19
* PSED–MR: 9, 10
* PSED–SCSA: 7, 9
* PSED–MFB: 3, 5, 13
* PD–HSC: 3
* UW–PC: 1, 6, 7, 8
* M–SSM: 1, 13

How old are we?

Equipment and resources

A large clear space. One practitioner to lead the activity and one more practitioner per individual child or small group of children. Family photographs or drawings for each child. (Ask for some to be brought into the setting, to be borrowed or copied and given back, or ask permission to take some at the setting when different family members bring or collect children, or ask for descriptions so that you may make symbolic drawings.) Ensure that each picture is labelled with a name and age and the relationship to the child. For example, Isobel, 17, Emily's sister or Eric, 73, Ted's grandad.

Activity

* Make time for each child to share and talk about their pictures with a practitioner on a one-to-one basis, to ensure that all labels are correct and any necessary extra information is understood by at least one adult, preferably the child's key person.

* Invite the children to work in small groups to compare families. Encourage them to take an interest in similarities and differences and celebrate diversity, to describe any special needs and disabilities and to include members of their extended families. Also respect a child's wish to include an important primary carer, such as a nanny or childminder, and others who have joined or become their family, such as stepfamilies or foster parents and siblings. Ensure that any discriminatory or unkind remarks are discouraged and that children understand how to be polite and careful not to upset others or hurt their feelings.

* Ask the child to decide whether their siblings or cousins are older or younger than themselves, whether their grandparents are older than their parents, who has the youngest baby in their family, the oldest sister, the youngest uncle or the oldest great grandparent.

* Some practitioners may choose to share some pictures and details of their own families with the children too.

Extensions

* Ask children if they can put their pictures together to show which people 'go together' because they are married or partners, such as Grandma and Grandpa, Mummy and Daddy or Auntie and Uncle. Some children may have two mothers or two fathers, called by different names or titles; some may have older siblings who have partners; some families may use their own names rather than titles. Check the correct pronunciations and meanings of titles used by families from different cultures.

* Working as a group, sort children's pictures into piles such as Mummies, Daddies, sisters, brothers, grandmothers, grandfathers and cousins. Support them as they look at the different people and understand that foster carers can be Mummies and Daddies too, siblings can be babies, children or teenagers and grandparents may be called by many different names.

* Challenge the group to order all of the pictures of children (under sixteen years) by age. They should find that their own ages form the longest lines or highest piles somewhere in the middle, but that there may be quite a lot of babies and toddlers who are younger and a mixture of older siblings.

Learning opportunities linked to Early Learning Goals

(See pages 8–13 for abbreviations.)

* CL–LA: 6, 9
* PSED–MFB: 5, 7, 8, 9, 12, 13
* CL–U: 2, 4, 5, 11
* UW–PC: 1, 2, 5, 6, 7, 8, 10
* CL–S: 3, 4, 13, 14, 15, 16, 18, 19
* M–N: 2, 3
* PSED–MR: 1, 7, 8, 9, 10
* M–SSM: 2, 3, 12
* PSED–SCSA: 6, 8, 9

Feelings

Equipment and resources

A large clear space. Three practitioners to lead the activity and possibly more practitioners to support the children. Three hand puppets – either people or animals who will speak as though they are human.

Activity

* Invite the children to sit as a group and watch the puppets. Create and act out a short scenario in which two puppets play a chasing game, then bump into each other and fall over. The third puppet should see what has happened, ask if they need help and go off to tell an adult.

* Ask the children how the characters were feeling at each stage of the story, whether the accident could have been avoided and whether they all behaved sensibly. Encourage them to talk about taking care when running, feeling sad or cross when they get hurt but accepting that sometimes accidents do happen. Discuss wanting to help each other, telling adults when they need help and feeling happy when people make things better.

* Create and perform another short act, during which two puppets are playing and a third asks to join in and is refused. The third puppet should display sadness and the others should then change their minds and welcome their friend into the game.

* Again, ask the children to name and describe the characters' feelings and how they should speak and behave towards each other so that nobody is sad. Emphasise that they may always ask an adult for help and support if somebody is not being kind.

Extensions

* Perform a scenario that begins with one puppet displaying sadness or anger. The other puppets should ask: Why are you sad / cross? Can I help? When the puppet replies with a reason, the others can ask the children to suggest solutions to the problem and act them out. For example: You could play with us. I'll help you to find the missing piece of your puzzle. You can share some playdough with me. I'll go and tell Joanna that you don't feel very well and she'll come and see you.

* If the group is ready and able to understand acting as pretending, develop disagreements and arguments between puppets and let the children suggest how to resolve them. Reassure nervous children that the puppets are being helped to learn better behaviour, so that they will stop feeling cross.

* Form groups, each of two children and one practitioner, and work together to create short role-plays using three puppets, to show to other groups. Encourage the children to offer ideas for theme and content and then to maintain a dialogue with the adult while pretending to be the puppet characters.

Learning opportunities linked to Early Learning Goals

(See pages 8–13 for abbreviations.)

* CL–LA: 6, 7, 11
* CL–U: 2, 3, 5
* CL–S: 4, 10, 11, 12, 13, 15, 17
* PSED–MR: 1, 5, 9, 11
* PSED–SCSA: 6, 8
* PSED–MFB: 4, 5, 11, 12, 13, 14
* EAD–BI: 1, 4, 8
* UW–PC: 3
* UW–W: 7

Story emotions

Equipment and resources

A large clear space. One practitioner to lead the activity and more practitioners to participate and support the children. A book or set of books containing illustrated fairy tales. Relevant props to assist in the acting out of some of the stories. A book or poster showing pictures of children expressing feelings and emotions.

Activity

* Share and discuss the stories and characters with the children as a whole group over several sessions. Make the books available in the reading area between group times, so that children may explore the stories individually and ask adults to read them to small groups again and again. Observe which are most popular.

* Choose well known and favourite parts of the stories and encourage the children to act them out, concentrating on the characters as they express their feelings and emotions. Offer props and resources to support the role-plays and encourage the actors to use their own words, movements and ideas. Help the children to take turns to act and to form an attentive audience for each other.

* Use blocks or cushions with hoods, hats or masks to explore hunger, anger, fear and then happiness in The Three Billygoats Gruff or Red Riding Hood. Use bowls, spoons, chairs and blankets to explore hunger, tiredness and surprise in Goldilocks and the Three Bears. Use a pumpkin, soft toys, a magic wand, a dress and shoes, or some beans or marbles, masks, play money and a stick to explore sadness, fear, anger and then happiness in Cinderella or Jack and the Beanstalk. The happy endings are very important to children of this age.

Extensions

* Show pictures of facial expressions from a book or poster and invite children to name them by asking: How does he feel? What is she showing us?

* Play a group game of making facial expressions to show various emotions and naming them. For example: Make your cross face! Show me your happy face! Invite children to share ideas of how emotions are caused and managed with the group, such as: I feel cross when I have to stop painting. I feel tired after lunch and I want to lie down and look at a book. I feel thirsty when I run outside and I need a drink of water. I feel sad when Mummy goes to work and happy when she comes back to me.

* Encourage the children to understand and label the most important feelings and emotions, in order to name and talk about them when they occur in daily life and therefore manage and control them more easily.

Learning opportunities linked to Early Learning Goals

(See pages 8–13 for abbreviations.)
* CL–LA: 1, 8, 11
* CL–U: 3, 5, 11
* CL–S: 8, 9, 10, 11, 12, 13, 15, 16
* PSED–MR: 5
* PSED–SCSA: 4, 6, 7
* PSED–MFB: 4, 5, 7, 9, 13, 14
* PD–MH: 2
* PD–HSC: 2, 4
* EAD–BI: 4, 5, 8
* L–R: 1, 6, 8, 10, 11, 13, 15, 16

Explanation of the development of speaking skills in children aged 4-5 years

This statement of age is only a rough guide, as all children are individuals and will acquire skills and develop abilities at different times and different rates.

Much will depend upon the experiences and stimulation that they receive from the environments and relationships provided by their homes and the early years settings and schools that they attend.

However, children are likely to acquire skills more or less in the following order, at the pace that is right for them.

● Using intonation and rhythm to make meanings clear.

● Talking about their own lives and families.

● Using a range of word endings and tenses correctly.

● Using connectives, including time words, to join phrases and create complex sentences when organising and sequencing events.

● Initiating conversations in order to form friendships with familiar adults and children.

● Pronouncing names correctly and speaking clearly and fluently.

● Expressing likes, dislikes and preferences and asking others whether they agree or differ.

● Inviting other children to join in with play, share or take turns.

● Beginning to understand that words should not be used to hurt others' feelings and wanting to say sorry when they have hurt or upset another child.

● Building up narratives and pretend sequences in role-play or small-world activities within a group, maintaining and extending play through offering ideas and discussing scenarios.

● Explaining own knowledge and understanding of why things happen and changes that occur and asking appropriate questions to find out more.

● Discussing stories, characters and detailed pictures within a group.

● Reminding themselves and others of rules, limits, unacceptable behaviours and possible consequences and developing the use of manners and social conventions.

● Using verbal skills to solve disagreements, find solutions, negotiate with other children and reach compromises.

● Speaking confidently to a familiar group of any size.

● Beginning to be able to speak confidently and politely to new people, such as a visitor to a setting, with the support of a familiar adult.

What are they doing?

Equipment and resources

A large clear space. One practitioner to lead the activity and more practitioners to support the children. A carefully chosen poster, frieze or big book or floor puzzle picture that depicts a busy scene involving lots of characters engaged in activities. An easel, stand, wall or display surface.

Activity

* Invite a group of children and practitioners to sit where everybody can clearly see the picture. Invite discussion on what is happening in the scene, offering some cues and prompts.

* Suggest that the group decides which season the scene is set in and what type of weather the characters are experiencing. Wonder aloud where the characters are, or where they have been, or where they are going. Talk about the possible relationships between characters in the picture. Invite comments about the emotions expressed within the picture, or how the children think that some of the characters are feeling and why.

* Support children in looking for clues and explaining what they think, rather than guessing, but accept all carefully thought-out ideas and explanations, even if you do not agree with the answers. Offer praise and encouragement to each child who displays imagination, creativity, logical reasoning or critical thinking and who speaks confidently to the group. Practitioners should introduce new words to extend children's vocabularies and enhance descriptive skills.

* Ask the group to decide whether they agree or disagree with various statements and promote an atmosphere of respecting each other's opinions and taking an interest in others' ideas.

Extensions

* Ask children to predict what might happen next to any of the characters in the picture, what any of the activities might lead to, and how different any of them might look. Or invite children to speculate on what might have happened just before the scene in the picture that might have led to some of the characters' actions or chosen projects.

* Encourage children to predict the effects of a dramatic happening or change. For example: if it started to rain heavily, it became very hot, it grew dark, a bridge collapsed, there was an accident, animals escaped from their enclosure or characters lost their way.

* Encourage children to talk about related experiences from their own lives, such as when they visited a similar place, took part in a similar project, or felt as the characters are feeling.

Learning opportunities linked to Early Learning Goals

(See pages 8–13 for abbreviations.)
* CL–LA: 6, 11
* CL–U: 4, 5, 11
* CL–S: 8, 10, 11, 12, 13, 19
* PSED–MR: 9
* PSED–SCSA: 6
* L–R: 11, 12

Thank you for coming

Equipment and resources

A large clear space. Enough practitioners to provide support for all children within the group. One or more visitors to the setting, who are prepared to speak on a topic of interest to the children, or read a story, or lead some singing or drama, or demonstrate a skill. (For example: a local police officer or vet, a teacher from a local primary school, a practitioner from another setting, or a parent who brings in a baby, cooks a snack or builds a shelf.)

Activity

*   Prepare the children in advance for each visitor. Discuss who the person or people will be, how to say their names and what they will do, demonstrate or talk about. Encourage the children to think in advance of questions they might like to ask.

*   Set up some role-play situations and model how to sit quietly and listen politely, how to participate within a group and how to speak to visitors. Encourage the children to take turns to pretend to be a visitor and to think how they would like to be treated at the setting.

*   Practise saying Hello, Goodbye and Thank you as a group and ask the children how they would like to express appreciation. They might give the visitors a clap, or sing a song, or make cards or drawings to give or send.

*   During a visit, sit and listen or join in with the children and support them in staying interested and focused. Create opportunities for them to ask their questions and monitor behaviour and levels of participation. Ensure that practitioners offer extra support to those children who need it.

*   After a visit, talk about children's home lives and whether anyone in their families do these jobs, enjoy these hobbies or care for animals or babies.

Extensions

*   Follow each visit by extending the theme, using stories, songs, small-world play and imaginative role-play, while the children's interest lasts. For example: introduce hospital play sets or turn the role-play area into a hairdressing salon or a part of the outdoor area into a fire station.

*   Provide opportunities for both children and practitioners to build upon the skills learned from visits. You might consider a pet for the setting or a trip to a farm to feed baby animals after meeting a vet, or offer dolls to care for or cookery or woodwork activities after a parent's talk or demonstration.

*   Support children in making their own books about the visits, encouraging them to remember the people involved and the sequence of events and to draw and attempt to write about their experiences.

Learning opportunities linked to Early Learning Goals

(See pages 8–13 for abbreviations.)

*   CL–LA: 11
*   L–R: 15, 16, 17
*   CL–U: 5, 11
*   L–W: 7
*   CL–S: 4, 7, 17
*   UW–PC: 6, 7, 9
*   PSED–MR: 5, 10
*   UW–W: 3, 6
*   PSED–SCSA: 2, 5
*   PSED–MFB: 9, 11
*   PD–MH: 9
*   EAD–EUMM: 3
*   EAD–BI: 1, 4, 8

Find the rhymes

Equipment and resources

A large clear space. One practitioner to lead the activity and more practitioners to participate and support the children. Books of simple rhymes and poems, CDs containing simple rhyming songs and picture books with stories told in rhyme. (Include some in each language spoken fluently enough by at least one practitioner.) Pencils and paper. Recording equipment.

Activity

* Read a simple rhyme or poem to the children, emphasising the rhyming words at the ends of the lines. Invite them to repeat it with you and to clap each time they say a rhyming word. For example: chant Incy Wincy Spider and clap as you say spout, out, rain and again. Read a selection of different lengths and types of poems and encourage children to repeat them, maintaining their rhythms and clapping at each of the rhymes as they hear them.

* Play some songs from a CD and encourage the children to listen carefully for rhymes. Support them as they sing the songs as a group, without the CD, aiming to recreate the tunes and rhythms and emphasise the rhymes by clapping and singing those words more loudly.

Extensions

* Use a picture book to read a rhyming story to the group. Emphasise the first word of each rhyming couplet and pause before the second word, allowing the children time to guess and call out what it might be. Note which children have grasped the idea of rhyme, which use context only to make sensible guesses and which need more support and practice to understand either or both of these concepts.

* Invite children to look for any books of poems or rhyming stories and any CDs of rhymes and songs that they have at home and bring them into the setting to share with the group. Value all contributions and include them in special circle or group times each day. Encourage parents' and carers' involvement, suggesting that they might write down or record their own or their children's favourites, in their first language, to give to the setting.

* Encourage children to create their own rhyming verses, stories and songs. Provide paper and pencils for them to write and draw their ideas and ensure that practitioners are available to support or scribe for them. Also provide access to recording equipment, so that they may record themselves and each other speaking and singing rhymes and play back their own voices.

Learning opportunities linked to Early Learning Goals

(See pages 8–13 for abbreviations.)
* CL–LA: 14
* CL–U: 2, 5
* CL–S: 13
* PSED–SCSA: 2, 6
* PD–MH: 5, 9
* EAD–EUMM: 7, 13
* L–R: 1, 2, 3, 4, 5, 8, 10, 16
* L–W: 2, 7
* UW–PC: 1, 10
* UW–T: 1

Round of sounds

Equipment and resources
A large clear space. One practitioner to lead the activity and more practitioners to participate in the game and support the children. Paper and pencils.

Activity
* Invite the children and adults to sit in a circle. Suggest a simple theme that everybody will understand, such as: things you can ride on, animals you can keep as pets or foods you can take on a picnic.

* Ask each person in turn to think of something connected to the theme beginning with a particular initial sound. Make the game fun for a mixed group by sensitively choosing simpler sounds for younger or less experienced children (often b, h, m, n, r, s, t), and more challenging ones for more confident children (maybe the vowels and f, g, l). Save the hardest sounds for the practitioners (such as j, q, v, w and c and k)!

* If any child struggles to think of a word, invite others to offer ideas to help. Repeat the most common sounds at intervals around the circle to allow for all of the children's ideas, such as: sandwiches, sausages, salami, scotch eggs and strawberries.

* As the group runs out of ideas, either end the game or change the theme and try another round of sounds.

Extensions
* Challenge the group to use their imaginations to come up with crazy and exotic ideas, instead of sensible ones, such as suggesting: anteaters, badgers, chameleons and dinosaurs as pets.

* Divide the children into small groups, each with one practitioner, and give each group a different intial sound. Ask them to think of as many words as possible connected to the theme that begin with their sound. The adults should encourage discussion and the sharing of ideas and write down the children's words, avoiding giving too many suggestions themselves (even if they do enjoy competing with their colleagues). They should then use the list to support and remind the children as each group in turn explains their words to everybody else.

* Give each child a pencil and paper and ask them to write down an idea, rather than speaking it, each time you suggest a sound and a theme. Encourage them not to call out. Reassure them that words do not need to be spelled correctly, but only recognisable to themselves so that they can read them aloud to the group. Display each letter as you call out its sound, so that all children may copy it to start their word. Those who cannot write other letters may draw pictures or symbols to record their ideas. Children will need varying degrees of support from practitioners.

Learning opportunities linked to Early Learning Goals
(See pages 8–13 for abbreviations.)
* CL–LA: 6, 11
* CL–U: 8
* CL–S: 5, 16, 18
* PSED–MR: 5, 8, 9
* PD–MH: 5, 9
* L–W: 4, 5, 6
* UW–W: 1, 5

© Debbie Chalmers and Brilliant Publications

Add a description

Equipment and resources

A large clear space. One practitioner to lead the activity and more practitioners to participate in the game and support the children. A large picture of an object that is easy to describe and that the children can relate to, such as: a bus, a cat, a tree, a car or a house.

Activity

* Invite the children and adults to sit in a circle and show them the picture. Allow a few minutes for everybody to look at, think about and discuss it. Name the picture clearly. For example, say: Here is a bus or whatever your picture is.

* Ask each child and adult in turn, around the circle, to add one more word to the description. They might say: Here is a red bus. Here is a big, red bus. Here is a big, tall, red bus. Here is a big, tall, shiny, red bus.

* Support children in repeating the sequence where necessary, so that they can insert their new ideas into the sentences in appropriate places. It is not essential that the adjectives are spoken in the same order every time, but it is easier to remember them if they are. Most new adjectives would be added after the others, but some words, such as colours, usually stay beside the noun in English and other adjectives are inserted before them, as in the example above.

Extensions

* Add verbs instead of adjectives, by asking players to imagine what the object might do. For example: Here is a bus that drives on the road. Here is a bus that makes a loud noise with its horn. Here is a bus that can splash through the rain. If appropriate for your group, encourage them to remember what others have said and add their own statement, creating a list, but, for many groups, making up one new statement each on the theme will be enough of a challenge at first.

* Ask the players to say whether they like the object in the picture or not, and why. For example: I like riding on the bus to go to the shops in the town. I don't like the bus because it splashes through all the puddles and makes the water fly up. I like the cat because it is soft and furry. I don't like the cat because it has sharp claws.

* Invite children to share their own experiences, prompted by the picture. They might describe their own cat or house, or talk about a journey made with their family on a bus or in their car.

Learning opportunities linked to Early Learning Goals

(See pages 8–13 for abbreviations.)
* CL–LA: 6, 9, 11
* CL–U: 2, 5
* CL–S: 2, 5, 8, 13, 14, 16, 18
* PSED–MR: 7
* UW–PC: 7, 8
* UW–W: 1, 4, 5

Speaking and Listening Activities for the Early Years
© Debbie Chalmers and Brilliant Publications

Will you be my friend?

Equipment and resources

A suitable play area within the setting, indoors or outdoors. At least six practitioners. Four favourite play activities, such as: playdough, painting, dressing up and wooden blocks.

Activity

* Ask one practitioner to sit at each activity. Select four confident children and invite each one to join a different adult. (Use your knowledge of individual children's preferences to choose a favourite activity to send each one to.)

* The other practitioners should now ask each child in the group to choose where they would like to play and suggest that they go to the activities of their choice.

* As each child approaches, the child already at the activity should invite them to play by asking a question such as: Would you like to play? Come and join in too? Do you want to play with me here? The adult may support both children in their responses, encouraging the visitor to reply with at least Yes please.

Extensions

* Ask children to find friends within the group and invite them to play a particular game. For example: Shall we play with the trains? Let's go outside to the scooters! Do you want to do some painting with me? Would you like to get the dollies out? Practitioners should be aware of any children who might not be chosen as friends and encourage others to seek them out.

* When two or three children are engaged in an activity, suggest to other children that they ask to join in. Support the children in accepting the newcomers and finding a way to share toys, materials or equipment. Encourage children to be polite but assertive and to understand what is fair. For example: We can each have four cars. Don't use up all of one colour; let's all have some red, some blue and some yellow. Share the play people or you'll have to stop playing with us.

* Encourage children to decide together how to take turns, making statements such as: I'll be first on the trampoline and then Amanda and then Bill; ten jumps each and we'll all count them together.

Learning opportunities linked to Early Learning Goals

(See pages 8–13 for abbreviations.)

* CL–U: 2, 4
* CL–S: 2, 4, 5, 7, 10, 13
* PSED–MR: 4, 6, 8, 9, 11
* PSED–SCSA: 1, 7, 8
* PSED–MFB: 5, 8, 9, 12, 13
* UW–PC: 4

Share with me

Equipment and resources

A large clear space. Two practitioners to lead the activity and more practitioners to support the children. Two hand puppets – either people or animals who will speak as humans. Small toys or play resources to be shared, such as cars, bricks, pens and paper or playdough. Table.

Activity

* Invite the children and adults to sit as a group and watch while two practitioners make the puppets perform a short play on the table. Choose a scenario that is relevant to the group and the setting, either because it already happens frequently or because you would like the children to move on to playing at that level. The puppets may share out four cars or ten bricks equally between them, take turns to draw with the different coloured pens or pull the playdough into two halves.

* Make the puppets talk about what they are doing, ask each other if they agree, use polite speech and good manners, negotiate, compromise and chat in a friendly way as they play. Encourage the children to participate by calling out ideas and suggestions and saying whether they agree with the puppets.

Extensions

* Act out minor disputes and disagreements between the puppets and ask the children to discuss the situations together and suggest ways that they could resolve their problems.

* Introduce a third puppet, operated by a third practitioner, and act out scenarios involving a child being invited to play or asking to join in with a game or activity when two children are already playing together.

* Make a collection of puppets available to the children and support them in creating their own scenes and short plays. Some of them may choose to perform to adults, friends or the rest of the group.

Learning opportunities linked to Early Learning Goals

(See pages 8–13 for abbreviations.)
* CL–U: 5, 11
* CL–S: 2, 7, 10, 13, 18, 19
* PSED–MR: 1, 5, 6, 7, 8, 9, 11
* PSED–SCSA: 1, 7, 8, 9
* PSED–MFB: 5, 7, 9, 12, 13, 14
* EAD–BI: 1, 4, 5, 8

Cycles of change

Equipment and resources

An outdoor area or a nearby park or garden where caterpillars and butterflies may be seen. One practitioner for each two children in the group. Magnifying glasses and bug viewing pots. Cameras that the children can use. A book or poster depicting the life cycle of a caterpillar/butterfly.

Activity

*   Read, discuss and explore the book or poster with the children and encourage them to imagine the two very different creatures and the change that occurs.

*   Search for caterpillars and help the children to examine them with magnifying glasses or to gently transfer them to bug viewing pots to look at them, to show them to each other and then carefully return them to the leaves on which they were found. Explain why it is important to be very gentle and careful with these small and fragile creatures and not to take them away from where they live and the food they eat.

*   Spot butterflies and show the children which plants attract them and how they settle on flowers and then fly away again. Look at them more closely through magnifying glasses if any stay still for long enough.

*   Support the children in taking photographs of the caterpillars they see and any butterflies they can snap in time, either on plants or in the air. Discuss and explore the book or poster again. Print out the children's photos and compare them with those in the book or on the poster.

*   Explain the life cycle and metamorphosis process carefully and invite the children to help you to describe what happens at each stage and remember key words, such as: egg, larva, caterpillar, pupa, butterfly.

Extensions

*   Act out the stages of the life cycle through music and drama. Encourage the children to curl up as eggs, wriggle as larvae, crawl as caterpillars, hang up as pupae and flutter as butterflies. Demonstrate for them the interesting bunching up and straightening out movement that some caterpillars use to move along the ground or a leaf.

*   Gather a collection of non-fiction and reference books and find pictures of many different types and colours of caterpillars and butterflies. Match them to each other and learn their names.

*   Explore other life cycles. Children especially enjoy learning about chickens, frogs and sunflowers. They may also be fascinated to find out about different sea creatures, birds and marsupials.

Learning objectives linked to Early Learning Goals

(See pages 8–13 for abbreviations.)

*   CL–U: 2, 5, 11
*   CL–S: 3, 8, 9, 15, 16, 18, 19
*   PSED–MR: 4, 8
*   PSED–SCSA: 4, 8
*   EAD–BI: 1, 5, 7
*   L–R: 11, 12, 15, 16, 17
*   UW–W: 4, 5, 6, 7
*   UW–T: 1, 2

What is happening?

Equipment and resources

A large clear space. One practitioner to lead the activity and more practitioners to support the children. A large poster or big book double-spread picture that shows a busy scene or characters involved in an activity or event. (Look out for pictures by illustrators such as: Richard Scarry, Quentin Blake, Debi Gliori, Shirley Hughes and Penny Dale.)

Activity

* Gather the children and adults into a group and invite them to study the picture quietly and think about what they can see. After a short time, invite comments and ideas by asking the question: What is happening? Depending on your group and the skills you want to encourage, either ask for children's contributions individually by name, or allow them to put up their hands and wait to speak, or to take turns in any other way. Ask practitioners for contributions whenever necessary, to extend the children's thinking or to introduce or clarify important concepts. Encourage children to relate the events in the picture to their own lives.

* Ask the group to consider: What happened before this? There may be many varying and some contradictory ideas. Ensure that the children understand that any of the ideas may be correct, because the answer is unknown. The fun is in the speculation.

* Move on to considering: What will happen next? Again, support children in understanding that many outcomes are possible and there are no right or wrong answers. Encourage every child to be confident enough to offer an idea or an opinion. Note which children think very logically and which enjoy the realms of fantasy. Make it clear to the group that both approaches are equally valued and may be useful in different situations.

Extensions

* Invite children in turn to pick out one character and describe him or her in detail. Encourage the others in the group to guess and point to the character being described.

* Ask the group to discuss numbers, quantities and comparisons within the picture. For example: How many children are wearing hats? Is there a lot of water in the pond? Are the kites flying higher than the trees?

* Encourage the children to decide, if they can, what season of the year the picture is showing, what time of day and what type of weather. Ask them to explain the clues that helped them to make their decisions. Outdoor scenes usually illustrate the season and weather more obviously, but it may only be possible to decide that it is day, evening or night time. In indoor scenes, the characters' clothes may be the only clue to the season or weather, but it can be easier to predict the time of day from their activities.

Learning objectives linked to Early Learning Goals

(See pages 8–13 for abbreviations.)

* CL–LA: 5
* CL–U: 2, 4, 5
* CL–S: 4, 8, 18, 19
* PSED–SCSA: 1, 8
* EAD–BI: 1, 6
* L–R: 11, 12, 13, 17
* UW–PC: 1, 5
* UW–W: 4, 5
* M–N: 1, 2, 6, 7
* M–SSM: 2, 3, 5, 6, 10, 12

Would you rather?

Equipment and resources

A large clear space. Three (or more) practitioners to lead the activity and more practitioners to support the children. Three (or more) mats, rugs or blankets. *Would You Rather?* the picture book by John Burningham (Red Fox).

Activity

* Share the book *Would You Rather?* with the children at a group or circle time, then invite your group of children to play the Would you rather? game. Sit on a mat as a group in the centre of the room or outdoor area. Ask two practitioners to sit on mats at the sides of the room or play area. Explain that you will ask a question and children should move to be with them at one side or the other according to their answer. For example: Would you rather eat fruit or vegetables? Fruit – sit with David; vegetables – sit with Debbie.

* When all of the children have chosen and are seated on a mat with a practitioner, ask them in turn to tell the group their preferences, supported by the adult if necessary. They might say: I would rather eat bananas, I would rather eat strawberries and grapes, I would rather eat carrots, I would rather eat potatoes and beans.

* Include a variety of popular themes, such as: toys, play activities, hobbies outside the setting, places to live, people to visit, transport, pets and clothes.

* Offer extra support to any child who appears to be just following a friend or the most popular choice, or always choosing the last option spoken, or moving at random.

Extensions

* Make the game more challenging by making the choices more similar, such as: Would you rather eat a sandwich or a roll? Would you rather draw with a pencil or a pen?

* Include comparisons of time and scale, such as: Would you rather go to bed early or late? Would you rather read a long story or a short one? Are you better at making models or quicker at puzzles?

* Set up three or four mats around the centre mat and offer more choices. For example: Would you rather use red, blue, yellow or pink paint? Would you rather see monkeys, tigers, penguins or snakes at the zoo?

Learning objectives linked to Early Learning Goals

(See pages 8–13 for abbreviations.)

* CL–LA: 9, 10.
* CL–U: 2, 4, 5, 9.
* CL–S: 8, 13, 14, 15, 16.
* PSED–MR: 5, 10.
* PSED–SCSA: 1, 2, 8, 9.
* PSED–MFB: 6, 9, 10.
* UW–PC: 5, 7

Sorry!

Equipment and resources

A large clear space. Two practitioners to lead the activity and more practitioners to support the children. A chair, a pen and paper, a few building bricks, an empty cup.

Activity

* Gather the children and practitioners to sit in a group and act out a few pretend situations for them. Walk backwards until you gently bump into each other and both say Sorry! Go to sit down on the same chair and the one who sits on it first says Sorry! I'll get another chair for you. Write a note with a pen while your colleague looks for one, saying I can't find my pen; say Sorry! I must have borrowed yours, but you can have it back now. Build a tower of bricks until your colleague tries to help and knocks it down, then says Sorry! Let's build it up again together. Knock over your colleague's cup and say Sorry! I didn't mean to spill your drink; I'll ask Jen to wipe it up and get you some more.

* Introduce non-accidental situations too. Say to each other: My drawing is better than yours. No, it isn't, mine's nice too! Sorry! Yes, they're both good, aren't they? and I don't want to play skipping with you today. But that's not fair, you said you'd play outside with me! Sorry! We could play skittles instead?

* Encourage the children to create similar role-plays in small groups, supported by practitioners. Invite them to perform for the group to watch if they would like to. If children learn the meaning of the word Sorry! in this way, they will understand how and why to use it and may begin to do so spontaneously at the setting. Praise all children for attempts to apologise to and negotiate with others.

Extensions

* Initiate a discussion with the group about how and when they say Sorry! with their families at home, taking careful note of all family members mentioned.

* Invite children who speak languages other than English to tell the group how to say Sorry! in their first or additional languages and encourage everybody to learn the words and practise saying them correctly. Encourage them to explain any differences in their home cultures surrounding the giving and accepting of apologies, if possible. Some cultures do not use words in this way, but children growing up and attending settings and public places must also learn how to observe the social conventions that are accepted in the country in which they live.

* Teach the children how to sign Sorry! and allow less confident children to begin by using the sign. Gradually encourage them to use the word too or instead, unless signing is their usual form of communication.

Learning objectives linked to Early Learning Goals

(See pages 8–13 for abbreviations.)

* CL–U: 2, 5
* CL–S: 6, 13
* PSED–MR: 1, 8, 11
* PSED–SCSA: 1, 3, 6, 8
* PSED–MFB: 5, 7, 8, 9, 10, 11, 13, 14
* EAD–BI: 1, 5, 6, 8.
* UW–PC: 3, 7, 10

What did they do?

Equipment and resources

A large clear space. One practitioner to lead the activity and more practitioners to support the children. A series of storybooks in which favourite characters face challenges and overcome obstacles.

Activity

* Read and discuss one of the stories with the group. Invite children to say how they think characters felt before and after each event and why. Encourage them to think in depth and develop their ideas by asking: Why did they do that? What did they think would happen? How did they feel when things went wrong? Would it have been different if they had remembered to wait? Should they have asked a friend or a grown up for help? Could they have been more careful?

* Share the other stories with the group in the same way, gradually, over a period of a week or two. Ask the children to think about whether the characters have learned any lessons, improved any skills, changed their behaviours or become better friends.

* Practitioners should model correct grammar and language at all times and help children both to extend the content of their statements and to speak more fluently, by changing tenses and word endings as appropriate.

Extensions

* Talk with practitioners and children about any times in their own lives that they have had to face similar changes or obstacles. Ask the adults to share some of their own experiences with the group and encourage the children to do so too, if they would like to.

* Provide small-world characters, vehicles, animals and other props and support children in re-creating some of the stories. Any toys may be used to symbolise the actual characters and their settings may be built from blocks or construction kits. Encourage children to speak for the characters, using dialogue that they remember from the stories and their own ideas.

* Offer paper and mark-making materials and support children as they make their own drawings, friezes or books to depict the stories. Encourage them to describe their sequences of pictures and support them in dictating or writing captions, at an appropriate level for each child.

Learning objectives linked to Early Learning Goals

(See pages 8–13 for abbreviations.)
* CL–LA: 9, 11
* CL–U: 4, 5, 11
* CL–S: 2, 4, 8, 10, 11, 12, 13, 15, 18
* PSED–MR: 9, 10
* PSED–MFB: 4, 5
* PD–MH: 9
* EAD–BI: 4, 8
* L–R: 8, 9, 10, 11, 12, 15, 16
* L–W: 2, 6, 7
* UW–PC: 1, 9
* UW–W: 3, 6

Hear the sound

Equipment and resources

A large clear space. One practitioner to lead the game and more practitioners to participate and support the children. An alphabet book, frieze or poster containing pictures that introduce each letter's phonic sound.

Activity

* Share the alphabet with the children as a group, encouraging them to listen carefully to each letter's phonic sound and the name of each picture and to repeat them with you. Draw their attention to the fact that, in English, c and k sound the same and some sounds rhyme or are very similar to each other, while others are quite different.

* When the children are familiar with the idea of the alphabet and the concept of each letter representing a different sound, introduce a game to reinforce their understanding and help them to remember which sound goes with each letter. Work on no more than four or five sounds at one session. Select each group of sounds to include some simpler ones that the children feel more confident with and one or two less familiar ones that they need to learn, such as: a, e, j, s and w. There is no need to follow alphabetical order; that may be absorbed separately by looking often at the poster or frieze and singing one of the well-known songs.

* Suggest simple topics and ask the adults and children to think of items beginning with the chosen sounds. For example: animals beginning with a – alligators, ants, alpacas; beginning with e – elephants, elks, echidnas; beginning with j – jaguars, jellyfish, jackals; beginning with s – snakes, sloths, salamanders; beginning with w – whales, walruses, wallabies.

* It may be necessary for practitioners to allow some very loosely connected words or to offer clues, as it is the initial sounds that are important to this activity and children need to feel that they can succeed in finding appropriate words. Return to the game regularly until you have covered the whole alphabet enough times.

Extensions

* Pronounce phonic sounds clearly one by one and invite children to come and point to the correct letters. Ensure that it is a game and no child will be afraid to guess or feel sad if they make a mistake. Each time a child points to the wrong letter, ask: Who else would like to try? until somebody guesses correctly, then say Well done to the two, three or more children together and ask them all to sit down again.

* Read some poems that rely on alliteration and encourage children to make up names for themselves, using their own initial sounds, such as: Smiling Susan, Careful Connie, Angry Alex.

* Suggest a theme, such as food, animals or things found in the garden. Offer the children an adjective and invite them to supply a relevant noun with the same initial sound, such as creamy cake or green grapefruit. The foods need not be realistic, but should alliterate – so melted cheese would not be correct, but melted meat would.

Learning objectives linked to Early Learning Goals

(See pages 8–13 for abbreviations.)
* CL–LA: 4, 9
* CL–U: 5
* CL–S: 2, 5, 16, 18
* PSED–MFB: 9, 13
* L–R: 4, 12, 17
* L–W: 4, 5

Model speeches

Equipment and resources
A large clear space. One practitioner to lead the activity and more practitioners to support the children. Models recently made by the children – from construction kits, blocks, clay, playdough or recycled and found materials. Camera and printer.

Activity
* Invite the children to show their models to the group in turn and to talk about them. Offer as much support as is needed by each child, encouraging them to say which materials and resources they used and in what order, how they assembled the models and fixed them together, how they decorated them and any names or labels that they have given to them.

* Encourage them to state whether they are representations of real objects or fantasy creations. They might say: This is a police car with wheels and a blue light on the top or It's a spaceship with aliens in it and it flies by magic.

* Ask the children whether they had any difficulties in making anything work or fix together and how they solved the problems. Encourage them to ask each other questions about the models. Ask whether they are pleased with their models and proud of them. Praise them for their modelling skills and their speaking skills and take a photo of each child and model.

* Print out the photos and put them into a book which children may keep in the setting and look at together whenever they wish. Consider also making a display board of the photos and some of the comments that the children made to share with parents and carers, as this can be a good talking point to encourage conversation between adults and children when arriving at and leaving the setting each day.

Extensions
* Make suitable cameras available to the children and encourage them to take photos of projects and games they are pleased with, such as paintings and drawings, playdough models, picnics, small-world scenarios, dressing-up costumes, role-play scenes and puppet shows. Ensure that you print out the photos at the end of each day and help the children to stick their own pictures into a scrapbook when they next attend the setting. Talk with them about the photos they have taken and support them in writing their names and any comments or scribe for them.

* Create models on a large scale with the whole group and display them for families and visitors to see. Take photos at all stages of the project and create instruction books for the children to keep and discuss.

* Encourage the children to try to create 3D models from more unusual materials, such as pipe cleaners and drinking straws, vegetables and matchsticks or wet sand, shells and grass.

* Share techniques such as papier mâché or weaving with wool. Talk about the properties of different materials and describe them.

Learning opportunities linked to Early Learning Goals
(See pages 8–13 for abbreviations.)
* CL–LA: 6
* EAD–EUMM: 12, 15
* CL–U: 4, 11
* L–W: 2, 6
* CL–S: 2, 4, 8, 9, 12, 13, 14, 15, 19
* UW–PC: 7
* PSED–MR: 8, 10
* UW–W: 1, 6
* PSED–SCSA: 3, 8, 9
* UW–T: 2
* PD–MH: 1, 4, 8.
* PD–HSC: 1, 4, 8

How speaking and listening skills contribute to the overall development of children aged 2-5 years

Prime area of Communication and Language

Listening and attention

Quality and quantity of language has a significant influence on a young child's ability to develop speech. The tone, the intention, the motivation and the emotion of the language heard is as important as the words. The amount and type of talk that goes on around a child affects his desire and ability to imitate and join in with it.

If shared experiences of language have been lacking at home or in a previous care environment, a child will need time and support to learn to engage and participate in the process of verbal communication. It is easier to teach a young child to direct and focus attention on specific areas that interest him and play experiences of his own choice, but he must also learn to take instructions where necessary, both for safety and for constructive and successful group participation.

Adults should aim to provide:

* An awareness of each child's verbal and non-verbal communication, to understand and respond appropriately when he is interested, excited, worried, soothed, bored, uncomfortable, tired, hungry, thirsty, hot, cold, etc

* Attentive listening and demonstrated interest in each child's attempts at communication, including non-verbal clues such as eye contact and body language, to encourage him to continue to develop his expressive skills

* A variety of experience, understanding and awareness of language usage, in order to give each child the best possible chance to engage in meaningful communication

* Positive attention, support, encouragement and praise for successful concentration, focusing and listening skills, which may result in taking turns, respecting others' right to speak, attempting to follow instructions or participating in a group activity.

Understanding

A child will be interested and motivated to acquire language that is useful, allowing him to express his needs, wishes and feelings or to contribute to conversations with special people, such as his key person and particular friends amongst his peers.

He may display different levels of competence at different times, as context changes a child's ability. Ensure that enough choice and opportunities are provided to attract the interest of every child, as some children prefer to describe, chant or learn facts while others prefer to fantasize and make up stories. A child may be very knowledgeable about a particular subject or topic and therefore be able to speak confidently and fluently with great enthusiasm when it is mentioned, but have no experience of another idea or theme and so contribute little to a discussion on that occasion.

Stories, poems, rhymes and songs, with rhythms and actions, can make language fun for all children, even when remembering and using speech effectively is still difficult for some. Including and sharing all languages spoken by families attending the setting, as well as signing, can build valuable relationships with parents and carers and encourage those learning more than one language to demonstrate their abilities in their home language, as well as the language spoken in the setting, and make significant progress in acquiring vocabulary and confidence in both. Sensitive prompts and cues, or visual aids such as pictures, photos, props, toys or puppets may also help to aid understanding.

Adults should support children in:

* Naming and describing the things that matter to them and the things that fascinate them and making links between their own experiences

* Talking about important events in their lives and learning that others within the setting may sometimes share them and sometimes have other experiences of their own

* Exploring and using new vocabulary while playing and extending their abilities to use a range of words, tenses and expressions confidently and appropriately

* Learning any routines, rules, boundaries and behavioural expectations that will enable them to function as a happy and successful member of the group within the setting.

Speaking

The frequency, type and quality of verbal interactions with adults and peers make a difference to a child's acquisition of speech, in terms of skill, fluency and self esteem. The adults' contribution is vital in the extending of vocabulary and variety of language. Speed, confidence and the ability to use correct grammar and master difficult sounds develop gradually through practice and repetition within a supportive and encouraging environment.

A child's attempt to speak or sign to communicate a verbal message should always be responded to positively and with encouragement – even when it is necessary to ask a child to please stop talking and listen while somebody else takes a turn to speak for a short time!

Adults should seek to offer:

* Shared positive experiences, as something to talk about is the best incentive for making an effort to find the words

* Time to chat in relaxed surroundings, on a one-to one basis and within small groups, modelling how to hold conversations by demonstrating interest and attention, asking and answering questions, offering related comments and taking turns to speak and listen

* Links to previous conversations, reminding children of similar experiences and situations or different reactions to significant events

* Opportunities to speak to a larger familiar group, to share special news from home or stories and descriptions of models, projects and play scenarios with others, at group, circle or snack times

* Access to stories, songs and rhymes, to be shared at different times with an adult, a small group and a larger group, to enhance listening skills and concentration, teach new vocabulary and the sound and repetition of language and encourage prediction and joining in

* Names and labels for everything, so that children may describe and talk about everything that is important to them, from the objects that they use and the colours, numbers and shapes that they see around them, to the emotions that they feel and the games that they play with their friends.

Prime area of Personal, Social and Emotional Development

Making relationships

Positive interactions, that allow children to exchange information, understand and care for each other, ask for help or offer it to others and make constructive relationships and satisfying friendships, rely on communication skills.

Understanding the routines and boundaries within the setting and being able to speak to others, in order to express needs, wishes and feelings, cope with changes or find out what will be happening next, enables a child to feel secure and able to safely explore and experiment, play and learn. If he is unable to understand and communicate effectively, due to a special educational need or disability, lack of proficiency in the language spoken within the setting, immaturity, underdeveloped speech skills, behavioural, emotional or social difficulties, he will suffer frustration and be unable to thrive.

Adults should encourage children to:

✱ Participate in group discussions and conversations, learning how to take turns to speak and to listen and to respect the ideas and opinions of all members of the group and their equal rights to talk and be listened to politely

✱ Notice, comment positively upon and ask appropriate questions about similarities and differences between people, to ensure that the setting is fully inclusive, valuing all cultures, preferences and special needs and celebrating diversity

✱ Interact with others in a positive and confident manner, observing the manners, social conventions and behavioural boundaries necessary to ensure the safety and well being of all members of the group

✱ Use conversation to make some particular friends, but also develop the confidence to speak to a variety of peers and communicate while engaged in activities with them, in order to recognise and promote themselves as important and popular members of the group.

Self-confidence and self-awareness
Children develop the self-confidence and self-esteem that they need to be happy and successful members of the community when they spend time with adults who praise them for their efforts and achievements, support and reassure them when they make mistakes and openly display that they take pleasure in their company. When they are offered opportunities to build on their own interests and make their own decisions and choices, they will be prepared to take risks in order to explore, experiment and learn. Speaking and listening to

each other is a vital part of these relationships.

Through chatting and positive verbal interactions, children learn to trust familiar adults to care for them, understand their needs, respect their preferences, set and adhere to fair and appropriate boundaries and inspire them to create satisfying play and learning experiences. They then feel secure and are able to extend this attitude to others, also seeking to earn trust in return by displaying high standards of language, ability and behaviour.

Talking through special or important events, occasions or situations can prevent possible worry, distress and loss of self-confidence for children, and, if they know how to ask for help or reassurance when they feel that they need it, they are more likely to cope with and enjoy new experiences. Using verbal explanations and visual aids, adults may prepare for these in advance, offer support while they are happening and provide follow up discussions afterwards, allowing children to voice their concerns and their pleasures and be valuable contributors to each experience.

Adults should understand that:

✱ Although some children enjoy leading or being the centre of attention, while others prefer to follow, to go their own way or to remain safely within the group, they all need encouragement to both speak and listen to others, in order to feel that they are valued contributors to the setting and to be able to make and keep friends

✱ Consistency and understanding the rules or sequences is of utmost importance to many people, so children may need to ask the same questions and receive the same answers over and over again, to feel reassured and safe before coping with a new experience

✱ It is through listening carefully to what children say, and what they don't say, that their carers may come to know how they see things (often very differently from adults), how much they understand, how much something matters to them and how they truly feel, so chatting in a relaxed way about feelings and experiences is important

✱ The gradual building of children's self-confidence and self-esteem contributes to their ability to be aware of themselves, others and their environment, so the way in which they are spoken to and the way in which they speak to each other must be carefully monitored and protected.

Managing feelings and behaviour

During a child's early years, he first develops enough self-awareness to believe that he is the centre of the universe, then moves on to understand that he is a member of a family and an educational setting and he should aim to fit in and contribute to the groups to which he belongs. He needs examples, advice and support to learn that others also have needs and equal rights to fulfil them. This task is easier when his speech, listening and understanding skills are well developed.

Sequences and routines help children to feel secure and confident and changes must be clearly communicated and explained in advance to avoid confusion, fear, anger or distress. Boundaries must be fairly enforced and as consistent as possible between settings and children's homes, so communication between practitioners and parents and carers is very important. An environment that provides a mixture of calm, quiet times and more exciting, stimulating periods will best meet children's needs for developing communication skills.

Adults must teach children how to talk (or sign) when they are frustrated, worried, sad, angry or upset, as well as when they are happy, excited or confused or have a physical need to address, such as tiredness, hunger, thirst, using the toilet or being too hot or cold. This will help to prevent the unwanted behaviours that can be caused by some of these feelings, such as tantrums, aggression, damaging toys and disengagement from the group. If feelings are strong, they may need to ask to leave the room or go indoors, or request a cushion that they may hit, or a ball that they may squeeze or throw. Symbolic role-play or small-world play, tactile materials or art and craft resources may also offer an outlet for a child who needs to express strong feelings and encouraging him to talk through the feelings or the problems while playing in this way can be even more helpful.

Children need to learn that they should never hurt other people and, within a supportive environment,

they can gradually absorb the concept of wanting to apologise or offer sympathy to another person, whether because of an accident, a deliberate act that they now regret, a loss of control or a situation that they have only observed or heard about. They may also learn to find their own solutions to problems and resolve conflicts verbally, if adults offer suggestions, rather than taking on the task for them, and much praise for successful outcomes.

Adults should help children to:

* Label and verbalise feelings and emotions, particularly anger and distress, in order to improve behaviour and self-control and begin to understand and support others who are struggling to do so

* Become aware of those around them and understand how their actions and attitudes affect other people and must be adapted to their situation, remembering that feelings and opinions are acceptable but verbalising them rather than reacting physically or explosively is expected

* Talk about appropriate or acceptable ways of expressing certain feelings and emotions during calm periods, in order to remember and use these methods independently, respond to verbal prompts and reminders or ask for help and support when necessary, to maintain control and safety and prevent damage and trauma

* Develop and use verbal skills to explain, understand, empathise, reason, negotiate and enthuse, in order to play and carry out projects successfully with friends and peers.

Prime area of Physical Development

Moving and handling

Children can absorb language more quickly when they use their whole bodies to respond to the instructions they hear and to create cooperative physical activities and games. Words are learned through movement and 'doing', especially verbs and adjectives, allowing children who have a vocabulary of nouns with which to name objects to make the transition to phrases, sentences and more fluent speech including descriptions and actions. Listening and concentration skills may be enhanced through games and activities which require children to wait for a signal, move or stop on cue, or take turns. Once a secure understanding of group participation and safety is in place, children may be encouraged to make up their own games and rules, contribute ideas, demonstrate and explain, negotiate with each other and describe their activities to adults within the setting or later at home.

Describing and explaining small-world play scenarios, acting out plays or using puppets, or demonstrating models made from craft resources or construction kits, to an adult or to the rest of the group, gives children a purpose and encouragement to use verbal skills to capture the attention of an audience. These can be further developed by inviting the audience to ask questions and supporting the children as they answer them. This combination of creative thinking and structured reporting, together with the fine motor skills involved in the projects, will contribute to the children's abilities to write independently.

Adults should provide opportunities for children to:

✱ Make and respond to play suggestions, using a combination of words and actions or movements while speech skills are at an early stage of development

✱ Challenge themselves to play group games co-operatively and to create extensions and variations of their own, using verbal and listening skills

✱ Explore language through understanding and carrying out sequences of actions and events, linking experiences and labelling processes, products, results and outcomes

✱ Continuously add new words to their vocabularies and create more complex sentences and descriptions by talking or writing about what they are doing, have done or are planning to do.

Health and self care

The gradual move from total reliance upon adults to developing some independence requires children to take increasing responsibility for personal needs. Although they will have communicated these to primary carers from the beginning, as they grow older they will begin to wish to make their desires for food, drink, sleep, hygiene or the use of the toilet known to other adults. To do this easily, they need to learn to speak or sign in a language understood within the setting. As speech becomes more fluent, they will be happier because they are able to state the specific help that they require, rather than asking in a more general way, and so develop or retain more independence.

A child will be able and eager to become more independent if he understands the reasons and rewards for doing so and the instructions and guidance that help him to achieve a task. For this reason, he needs to develop adequate listening skills and the ability to absorb information, along with the confidence to ask questions when he is unsure. Within a consistent and fair environment, he can learn that others have both similar and differing needs and, through talking to them, offer understanding, support and empathy.

Once listening, speech and language skills are well developed, children can share conversations and stories with adults to learn about a healthy diet, the importance of exercise and rest and how to keep themselves safe and talk about these issues with their families at home.

Adults should enable children to develop independence by:

✱ Giving them the words they need to name and describe their personal needs and the help they would like at different times

✱ Listening carefully to what they say and rewarding their attempts to communicate clearly by providing exactly what they ask for, or an appropriate and available item or experience that is as similar as possible

* Praising every small step and effort that they make towards the recognising and taking care of their own personal needs without help or reminders

* Offering them relevant information and ideas and then opportunities to make choices and decisions for themselves, within safe boundaries.

Specific area of Expressive Arts and Design

Exploring and using media and materials

Expressive and performing arts rely on speaking and listening skills, as people need both to express themselves in a way that others can understand and to listen to others, in order to work in a team and achieve projects and effects cooperatively.

Children need to learn to listen and distinguish between sounds, so that they may appreciate music, songs and rhythm and begin to create movements and dances and play instruments. They need speech or signs so that they may name the movements they choose to make or the instruments they would like to use, describe their dances and tunes and sing familiar or invented songs. The ability to work within a team or group may be learned and developed through many enjoyable musical games, but children first need to understand how to listen to and discuss the rules and how to respond to the cues given by the music or other players.

When children are engaged in art and craft work or other creative and imaginative projects, their development and their enjoyment of the activities are enhanced if they can chat about what they are doing with adults and friends and share descriptions, demonstrations, explanations and ideas. Putting their experiences into words may also help them to remember what worked well or didn't work on previous occasions and manipulate materials and resources with more confidence. Being able to name colours and textures, talk about properties, predict outcomes and link cause and effect enables children to talk, interact, play

and experiment on a higher level, continuously adding new vocabulary and learning how to use comparisons and identify similarities and differences.

Adults should contribute to development by:
* Using the correct names for materials, instruments, movements and activities and also encouraging children to make up their own words to label and describe their creations, to extend their vocabularies and enhance their language skills

* Modelling techniques and ideas alongside children as they work with materials and resources and chatting with them about other similar projects that have been followed or may be planned for the future

* Asking open questions to prompt children to continue with imaginative ideas and extend their thinking as far as possible, and making suggestions to maintain their enthusiasm and abilities to solve problems through creative thinking, when difficulties might have made them give up

* Sharing delight, wonder and awe when discoveries are made or unexpected outcomes occur and telling children that nobody ever stops learning and that there are no right or wrong answers in creativity.

Being imaginative

Engaging in satisfying pretend play, whether through dressing up, using small-world figures, presenting plays and stories with puppets or taking part in drama, allows children to use their minds and bodies together and to develop the imaginative skills that they will need for confident group work, extensive reading and interesting writing throughout their school lives and beyond. Adults may set a good example by displaying a high degree of interest in the children's creative ideas, and also help to extend the ideas further by offering new concepts, resources and experiences that will appeal to them as individuals and groups.

Children need to talk and listen in order to tell stories, speak in character, contribute, agree and share ideas, negotiate and find solutions and compromises. When they can do this, they can form constructive relationships with peers and continue and maintain play experiences together. Making friendships in this way allows children to develop the social confidence to express their own ideas, theories and fantasies, join in with or lead a group and enjoy conversations.

Adults should make it possible for children to:

* Easily and independently access the resources and equipment that they need to carry out or develop any of their ideas, asking an adult for support in reaching and lifting heavy and awkward items or providing more supplies or appropriate alternatives when materials are already in use or used up

* Feel confident that they may move, adapt and transport items of furniture and play equipment if they need to use them in a different area or combine them with others to create a desired effect

* Enjoy a wide variety of books, small-world figures, animals, vehicles and accessories, toys and items for role-play, dressing-up outfits, construction kits, messy and tactile activities, stories, rhymes and songs on CDs, soft toys and puppets with which they may develop imaginative scenarios and sequences and tell their own stories

* Explore and imagine situations and emotions relevant to their own lives, both those that they have experienced and those which have not yet happened to them, in order to address worries and fears, make sense of relationships and events and develop empathy for others

* Choose, build and strengthen friendships at their own paces and appreciate the value of being a member of a group or community, getting on with others and enjoying the company of special people.

Specific area of Literacy

Reading
When adults share books, stories, poems, rhymes and songs with children, they hear and absorb the richness of language, long before they can distinguish or imitate all of the separate words or understand what they mean. A love of the sound and pattern of words gives children an incentive to listen to others talking and to explore the uses and pleasure of speech for themselves. Practising words, phrases and intonation through joining in with favourite stories, songs and rhymes increases children's fluency and enunciation and gives them an incentive to want to learn to read for themselves.

A continuing emphasis on speaking and listening skills once independent reading begins encourages children to recognise rhymes, phonic sounds and alliteration and use them as clues to help in deciphering words and sentences. If letter names and sounds and the words they create are familiar and securely understood, they may attempt to read anything with confidence. Being able to hear and recognise subtle differences between sounds and inflections will help them both with reading and with speech, in more than one language if opportunities arise.

Children who are already proficient in description and conversation will find context and meaning within the words they read, allowing them to progress more quickly. Including dialogues and expressions and using different or funny voices for characters ensures that reading remains fun and that children feel that they are controlling the words and mastering the skills, rather than being overwhelmed by the task of learning to read.

Adults should invite children to enjoy language through:

* Providing a range of attractive and interesting books and other reading matter (both fiction and non-fiction) and changing the selection frequently enough, while ensuring that established favourites are always available

* Being prepared to give time and enthusiasm to reading whenever a child would like to

share it, either by reading aloud or supporting shared or independent reading skills

* Setting the example throughout the setting of promoting and valuing listening, speaking, reading and singing and attaching importance to these activities, giving both specific and spontaneous periods of time to them and demonstrating the benefits and enjoyment that they can bring

* Chatting, telling stories, relating experiences, creating narratives for drama, role-play and imaginative play scenarios, playing with words and sounds through games and activities and exploring many languages.

Writing

When children have interesting experiences to talk about and are encouraged to create imaginative games, they often want to record their ideas and memories with pictures, photographs and models. They can be encouraged to describe, display and share their artistic work through mark making and dictating words for adults to scribe for them.

If the recording experiences are positive and lead to others showing an increased interest in what they have to say and rewarding them with praise and attention, children will begin to enjoy using letters and words to put together phrases and sentences. As soon as they are ready, they will ask for support in learning to write their own names and labels for their drawings and displays. This will, in turn, lead to more talking, explaining and imagining and further develop the speaking and listening skills needed for successful conversations and for speaking confidently to a familiar group.

Adults should be alert and tuned into children's needs so that they may:
* Provide materials and resources, time, opportunities and incentives for them to want to begin to make marks that they call writing and encourage them through talking about their pictures and models and suggesting names, words and simple phrases to label them

* Offer support and encouragement at all stages of the process of moving from early mark making, through tracing, copying, guessing and memorising letters, learning initial sounds and developing phonic awareness, to independent writing, using a variety of paces and approaches to suit individuals

* Use writing at every opportunity and draw their attention to its usefulness, by involving them in making lists and notes as reminders, letters to explain events and requests to parents and carers, displays for everybody to enjoy together and individual projects such as notices, storybooks and scrapbooks

* Challenge them to recognise familiar words on toys and packaging, books and posters and in the environment, talking about why different sizes and fonts are used to make writing more interesting and how these can be used when creating speeches for different characters or emphasising certain words or sounds.

Specific area of Understanding the World

People and communities

To be able to appreciate the society that we live in today and develop a wider knowledge of the world and its people, children need to be able to absorb and exchange information. They should learn about similarities and differences between families, cultures, beliefs and communities and understand that, since many people now travel or emigrate and do not live in their country of birth or origin, settings may include a diverse selection of people. Care must be taken to ensure that settings include multicultural toys, books, posters, music and resources and that all families feel welcome and valued within the group. Talking and listening to each other encourages everybody to respect all needs, feelings and opinions equally and to take an interest in events, celebrations and experiences that may be shared.

It is very important to listen carefully to the pronunciations of names and key words in children's and families' first languages, when they first join a setting, and to ask them to repeat them several times at first if necessary, to ensure that the adults can say them correctly. They may then support the children in learning and saying each other's names and beginning to speak to each other positively, as well as feeling confident to speak to parents and carers and to chat with children about their families using their names.

Special and additional needs and disabilities may also be discussed, explained and explored through information books and stories provided children have the concentration skills to listen and understand and the language skills to talk about what they have heard, to ask questions and to make connections with people that they know.

Adults should talk with children about:

* Understanding that all people are not the same but that all people are important, so they should be treated not in the same way but with equal respect, which may mean making allowances for differences, adapting equipment, games or speech, offering extra support or patience, being flexible or embracing new experiences

* The importance of finding ways to communicate with others and to pay attention to what they may be saying, even if they are unable to use a spoken language or the one usually spoken within the setting

* The people who help us within the community and the important messages that they have to give to us on issues of health, safety and behaviour

* Special occasions and festivals, especially those celebrated by the families attending the setting, and when, why and how they are important to and shared by groups of people.

The world
When children have opportunities to explore and experience the natural world and their local environment, they will have questions that they want to ask and observations that they want to make. If they travel to other places with their

families or carers, they should be encouraged to observe them carefully and describe them to the group after their return.

They will enjoy describing their experiences and feelings about trips, remembering what they did and saw and explaining their observations and ideas to adults and friends. Adults may support this by offering new words as names and labels for some of the things they describe, helping them to link their new experiences with other similar ones that they have encountered in the past and by encouraging them to speak individually and to listen to each other politely.

Adults should take every opportunity to:

* Encourage children to talk about their own experiences, observations, ideas and theories by being attentive listeners and supporting other children to form an appreciative audience, ensuring that all children who wish to speak have a chance to do so and to be Equally and fairly listened to and that all take a turn in listening to others

* Increase children's vocabularies and enhance their language skills by offering new words and descriptions, asking questions that require deeper thinking or detailed answers, pretending not to understand to challenge them to explain more clearly and suggesting ideas that are obviously wrong to keep the conversation fun and amusing

* Enhance children's understanding of changes that occur, whether they can be influenced, why certain things happen and how some things work by encouraging them to make comparisons and wonder 'what if'

* Talk about potential dangers and ways to keep safe and the importance of being aware and alert, asking children to explain familiar safety policies, procedures and the reasons for them to check their listening skills and levels of understanding.

Technology

The ability to speak and listen effectively allows children to follow instructions and understand safety rules before attempting to operate equipment. Being able to access and use such resources as computers, cameras, calculators, CD players and remote controlled toys independently offers them a wider and more exciting choice of free play within a setting. They may also develop the confidence to use their skills and similar equipment at home, such as speaking on the telephone to grandparents or family members who are away from the home, choosing and playing CDs, accessing simple games and activities on a computer or taking photographs of their family.

When explaining how to use resources or play games, adults may accompany their speech with demonstrations and ask children questions or invite them to explain to others to check that they have listened and understood.

Adults should challenge children to:

* Describe their own actions and discoveries and put forward theories and creative ideas to explain why some actions cause certain things to happen to different resources and what might happen if they alter what they do or use

* Give instructions, as well as follow them, so that they may practise choosing words carefully and producing clear speech that will not confuse their listeners

* Develop critical thinking and use logical reasoning to decide how some pieces of equipment work and how they may be operated in order to achieve various outcomes and results

* Create a particular effect or achieve a desired outcome using any methods and resources that they wish, working alone or with a partner or within a group, and then to describe and explain the process, the discoveries, the decisions and the results that occurred along the way.

Specific area of Mathematics

Numbers

Children hear numbers all around them and can enjoy learning number names and chanting them from an early age, although a true understanding of counting and using numbers develops a little later. They gain simple numeracy skills and confidence through sharing counting rhymes and songs, number books and games with adults and groups of peers. They can absorb the sounds of number names in many languages, while recognisng that their signs and quantities, and often numerals, do not change, so sharing number songs, chanting and counting can be an ideal way to introduce them to the concept of people speaking and using different languages.

Concepts of number may be introduced through talking about experiences that are real and relevant to the children, such as their ages, how many pieces of food they eat at snack time or how many children are playing in a particular area. They may begin to understand comparisons and descriptions by chatting about who has built a tower using most bricks, who has had more or less milk to drink from the jug or which sides of dice have more or fewer spots. Visual reminders, such as pictures and numerals on posters and displays, will reinforce understanding alongside the speaking and listening.

Adults should increase children's awareness of numbers by:

* Including them in everyday activities, such as counting steps while walking or climbing, counting aloud in games of hide and seek and spotting numerals on toy boxes and packaging

* Commenting on basic similarities, differences and comparisons, such as two eyes and two ears but one nose; three 4-year-olds and two 3-year olds; or five children and one adult at each table

* Introducing one-to-one correspondence through providing two boots for two feet, one plate for each soft toy at a pretend picnic or one engine for each child playing with the

railway track

* Playing at chanting and singing numbers in different ways, such as forwards and backwards, speaking alternate numbers in pairs or having one group echo another in the same or a different language.

Shape, space and measure:

Shapes hold a fascination for most children and the ability to name or describe them, fit them together and select the right ones for different purposes are important skills to develop. The names of the most common and regular shapes can be taught through the many books, posters, games, puzzles and musical instruments available, as well as specific mathematical equipment, and children should be encouraged to explore both 2D and 3D shapes. Describing them will involve both logical and imaginative vocabulary and careful listening and thinking will allow them to guess which ones an adult is describing. Sizes and weights of objects may be introduced in the same way.

The imaginative possibilities of small-world play allows children to create shapes and spaces, compare sizes and weights and measure distances. Messy play, with tactile materials, and art, craft and model making, with a variety of resources, encourage them to use their knowledge of shapes and sizes and their experiences of measuring to experiment with the ways in which they can relate to or affect each other. Other activities, particularly cookery, science and gardening projects, can successfully introduce the concept of time and how to measure it in a variety of ways.

Adults should enhance children's interest in mathematical concepts by:

* Talking about shapes and sizes whenever possible and drawing attention to examples of both regular and unusual shapes and extremes of size

* Encouraging children to describe the spaces and distances left between items and to think of creative ways to compare, measure and record them

* Drawing attention to sequences, routines and short periods of time and helping children to find ways of measuring and recording how long it takes to do something, how quickly they can complete a task or how long they must wait until something happens or is finished or ready

* Inviting imaginative descriptions of objects, materials, pictures and models that allow them to truly understand how something looks, feels or behaves by talking about it using words that they understand and relate to, supplying labels and extending vocabulary further in ways appropriate to individuals

* Introducing humour and jokes into descriptions and discussions to stimulate quicker thinking or a deeper understanding, such as asking whether an elephant painted on the fence outside might suddenly grow enormous and try to walk in through the door, or who would like to go for a ride in the model rocket to explore space and search for alien friends.

© Debbie Chalmers and Brilliant Publications

Listen to each other

Equipment and resources

A clear space with room for the group to sit quietly together. One practitioner to lead the activity and more practitioners to support the children.

Activity

* Work with a small group of four or five children. Ask a simple and specific question, such as Did you walk or drive here today? or Do you like apples, pears or bananas best? Ask them all to think of their answer inside their heads or whisper to themselves and not call out. Invite each child by name to give their answer in turn, encouraging the others to wait and listen. For example: Please listen everybody, while we ask Olivia – Did you walk or drive today? Now let's all listen and ask Evan – Did you walk or drive today? Well done for waiting Ella; now it's your turn to tell us – Did you walk or drive today?

* Gradually increase the size of the group, as the children become more used to waiting and taking turns. Ensure that every child always has a turn to speak and change the order with each question, so that any child may speak first, last or somewhere between. Ask other practitioners to sit with those children who need extra support in waiting and listening. Offer lots of praise to all of the children for speaking and listening carefully to each other.

Extensions

* Make the questions more open ended and requiring deeper thinking. For example: Which is your favourite colour to mix with the paints? What would you choose to buy from the shop for lunch?

* Invite children and practitioners to sit in a circle. Turn to the child beside you and ask a question, encouraging everybody to listen carefully to the answer. Suggest that the child then turns to the next person and asks the question and that this continues around the circle. Everybody should listen while they wait for their turns to speak.

* Demonstrate how to make a statement and follow it with a question, in order to initiate a conversation, such as: I go swimming with my brother. Do you like swimming? Support children in developing this skill in pairs, first working with a practitioner, then with a friend.

Learning opportunities linked to Early Learning Goals

(See pages 8–13 for abbreviations.)

* CL–LA: 5, 6, 11
* CL–U: 2, 4
* CL–S: 1, 3, 6, 14
* PSED–MFB: 9, 10, 11, 13
* UW–PC: 6, 7, 8

Me please!

Equipment and resources

A large clear space. One practitioner to lead the activity and two practitioners to participate and support the children. Two or more popular activities that are often provided within the setting.

Activity

* Ask two practitioners to stand in separate spaces. Ensure that all of the children know their names. Explain a simple choice to the children, such as: they may go outside or stay inside to play, or they may listen to a story or build with blocks.

* Speak to the group, asking: Who wants to go outside? or Who would like to hear the story? Encourage the children to choose by nodding or raising a hand or standing up while saying: I do please! or Me please! or making signs to indicate yes or me and please.

* Invite those who indicated yes in this way to stand with one practitioner: Could those people please go to stand with Alison? Invite the others to indicate no and choose the other option by moving to the other practitioner: If you want to play inside or If you'd like to build with blocks, please could you go to stand with Theresa?

* If any children do not move to a practitioner, ask them again individually and, when they do indicate their choice, support them in joining the appropriate group.

* Praise all children for choosing sensibly and reward them by providing their chosen activities immediately.

Extensions

* Offer three or four choices instead of two. Ensure that the children listen to and consider them all before choosing, as many may tend to call out Me! to the first suggestion when they would actually prefer another.

* Use the same technique to encourage children to think about and remember their own needs. For example: Who needs to use the toilet before tea? Who is going home for lunch today? Who would like to fetch a toy from their bag for sleeptime?

* Encourage good manners and cooperation at the table at meal or snack times by asking: Who would like another sandwich? Who would like some custard? Who would like some more water? and passing plates and jugs.

Learning opportunities linked to Early Learning Goals

(See pages 8–13 for abbreviations.)
* CL–U: 4, 8, 9
* CL–S: 1, 6, 14, 21
* PSED–SCSA: 1, 2, 3, 8
* PSED–MFB: 1, 9, 13
* PD–HSC: 2, 3
* EAD–EUMM: 1

Which one do I mean?

Equipment and resources

A large clear space. One practitioner to lead the activity and more practitioners to support the children. One or more pictures or posters depicting animals, vehicles, fruits, plants, mini-beasts, places, story characters or any topic of interest to the children in the setting.

Activity

* Gather the children and adults as a group and invite them to sit where they can all see the poster clearly. Describe one of the pictures, a little at a time, and invite the children to listen carefully to try to guess which one you are talking about and to call out its name as soon as they think they know the answer. For example: It's an animal. A big animal. A big grey animal. It has big ears. Its tail is small. It lives in a jungle or a zoo ...

* As soon as any children guess and name the picture correctly, ask them to point to it on the poster, so that all of the children are sure of the answer. Then offer clues to a different picture. Adjust the complexity of the clues to suit the group's experience and concentration levels. When nobody can guess, offer a rhyming word or initial sound clue.

* Continue with the game for as long as the children's interest and concentration lasts. If it is popular, play it often, using differently themed posters.

Extensions

* Take the posters down and challenge the children to play the game with no visual clues. Begin by describing pictures from the posters, that the children have seen, and move on to other ideas that they must imagine from their own experiences.

* Invite children to take turns to give clues to the group by describing a picture on a poster. A child of this age will need the support of a practitioner to secretly choose a picture, think of enough clues and not give away the answer too soon!

* Challenge the group to think of as many answers as possible, instead of one, by asking them questions such as: How many red fruits can you think of? or Which animals have fur?

Learning opportunities linked to Early Learning Goals

(See pages 8–13 for abbreviations.)
* CL–LA: 9, 11
* CL–U: 1, 2
* CL–S: 3, 8, 14, 16, 18, 20
* PSED–MR: 5, 7
* L–R: 4, 12, 13, 15, 17
* L–W: 4, 5
* UW–W: 4, 5

What happened to you?

Equipment and resources

A clear space. One practitioner to lead the activity and another practitioner where necessary to support a child with additional needs. Children's own postcards, photographs or special items from home. An illustrated brochure or photographs of a place that is popular amongst the children's families and visited by many of them.

Activity

* Work with two or three children at a time, on whichever day of the week they first attend the setting. Talk to them about what you did at home with your family at the weekend and invite them to tell you about their experiences in return. Support them with prompts, such as: Who did that with you? Where did you go on your scooter? How did you bump your knee? What did Granny make for lunch? How do you say 'swimming' in your language with Mummy?

* When you have talked with them all, bring together children who have expressed similar interests or experiences, such as those who often go to the local park on their scooters, those who go swimming on Saturdays or those who visit grandparents on Sundays, and encourage them to chat with each other.

Extensions

* Repeat the activity after a holiday, during which the setting was closed, and encourage the children to remember one or two special things that they did with their families or carers a week or two ago. Suggest that they might bring in postcards, photos or other items to help them to explain to the group. Bring together friends and siblings within the setting and support them as they describe to the group something that they have done together.

* Choose a popular place that as many of the children as possible are familiar with. Obtain an illustrated brochure or some photographs of the place. Introduce the place to the group with some of your own observations and thoughts. Invite each child in turn to tell everybody something about the place. Encourage them to look at the pictures and remark on any signs, using words or symbolic drawings, that they recognise, such as: swimming pool, toilets, roadworks, pelican crossing, Danger or Stop.

Learning opportunities linked to Early Learning Goals

(See pages 8–13 for abbreviations.)
* CL–LA: 6, 9
* CL–U: 3, 4, 11
* CL–S: 2, 3, 4, 13, 15, 18, 19
* PSED–MR: 5, 8, 10
* PSED–SCSA: 1, 6, 9
* L–W: 1
* UW–PC: 2, 6, 7, 8, 9, 10

If I feel cross

Equipment and resources

A large clear space. Two practitioners to lead the activity and more practitioners to support the children. Toys and musical instruments for role-plays. Puppets or soft toys. Small-world figures and toys. Large sheet of paper and marker pen.

Activity

* Gather the children and adults into a group. Demonstrate the emotion cross, using facial expression and body posture. Ask the children if they know how you are feeling when you look like that. Repeat with other emotions, such as: sad, worried, happy and excited. Encourage the children to repeat the words as they copy the expressions.

* Role-play some simple mimed scenarios with another practitioner and emphasise the emotions you are both expressing. In your first act, be happy while you are building up blocks, until your friend becomes too excited and snatches one, knocking them over. Then be cross and snatch the block back, making your friend sad. In your second act, play a tambourine very loudly while your friend covers their ears with a worried face, then notice the expression and play more quietly until your friend is happy and joining in.

* Invite the children to talk about what you could do to make things better, encouraging them to think of expressing their emotions verbally, instead of using physical force or a tantrum, crying or staying worried.

* Role-play the scenarios again including speech and solutions. Say: I feel cross because the blocks fell down! and I'm sorry, let's build them up again together. or That noise makes me feel frightened! and We could play together more gently.

Extensions

* Offer puppets or soft toys and encourage children to teach them how to talk to each other when playing together or sharing toys.

* Develop role-play scenarios with small-world figures and ask children to help you to find solutions to their problems.

* Support the children in recognising their own emotions and creating a list of strategies to use when they feel too cross, sad, worried or over-excited. They might say the feeling out loud, count to five, take a deep breath, walk away or talk to an adult. Write out these ideas for the children and display the list for parents and carers to see. Encourage the children to use the strategies at home as well as in the setting.

Learning opportunities linked to Early Learning Goals

(See pages 8–13 for abbreviations.)
* CL–U: 2, 5
* CL–S: 4, 8, 10, 13, 17
* PSED–MR: 1, 11
* PSED–SCSA: 1, 7
* PSED–MFB: 1, 3, 4, 5, 7, 8, 12, 14
* PD–HSC: 1, 2
* EAD–BI: 4, 6, 8

Find it

Equipment and resources

An indoor or outdoor area of the setting full of appropriate toys and resources. One practitioner to lead the activity and more practitioners to support the children.

Activity

* Sit with a small group of children in the middle of a room or outdoor area and encourage them to look around them in all directions to see what is there. Describe something that you can see and invite them to guess what it is. Gradually offer one clue at a time until it is guessed correctly.

* Ask the child or children who guessed and named the item first to go and touch or point to it, then to sit down beside it. Ask only the children left in the group in the middle to guess the next item and move to it, until no children are left there. The last children to guess may need very simple clues or the support of a practitioner.

* Invite each child or small group of children in turn to give you clues, so that you can try to find the objects that they are describing.

Extensions

* Give each child a different colour and ask them all to find as many objects as possible in that colour, then to come back to the group and try to remember and name them all. Count together how many of each colour were found.

* Repeat this game, giving each child or pair of children an adjective instead of a colour, such as: big, small, tiny, thin, round, soft, heavy and shiny.

* Involve the children in fetching objects for each other as a game. Ask one child: Matthew, please find something yellow for Gary. Tim, please find something shiny for Chrissie. Encourage them to speak to each other, saying: Here you are Helen, it's a beanbag for you. Thank you, Duncan.

Learning opportunities linked to Early Learning Goals

(See pages 8–13 for abbreviations.)
* CL–U: 1, 2, 5, 6, 8
* CL–S: 1, 8, 21
* PSED–MR: 5, 7
* PSED–SCSA: 2, 4
* M–N: 2, 4, 8
* M–SSM: 2, 10, 11

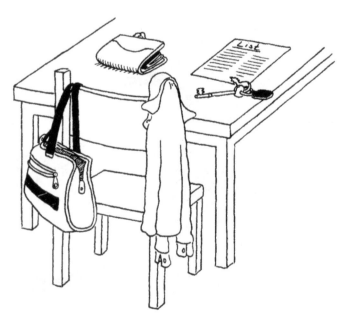

Speaking and Listening Activities for the Early Years

I like that

Equipment and resources

A large clear space with a safe ground or floor surface for movement. One practitioner to lead the game and more practitioners to participate and support the children. Large paper circles in a variety of colours.

Activity

* Decide on a theme, such as breakfast foods, and make a statement as you walk to stand in a space: I like eggs for breakfast. Prompt each of the other practitioners in turn, by name, and they should either say: Yes, I like eggs for breakfast and join you, or say: No, I don't like eggs for breakfast and walk to another space. When all of the adults have spoken, invite each of the children in turn to make their statement and join one of the groups.

* One of the adults in the No group should then walk to another space, making a different statement, such as: I like toast for breakfast. Each adult and child in turn may make their statement beginning with Yes or No and form two groups again.

* Repeat the game until nobody can think of any more ideas for the theme.

Extensions

* Ask the children to go to stand on the circle of their favourite colour and shout out: I like (pink) best! Talk about which colours are most popular. Remove all but the two most popular colours and ask the children to choose again, then speak in unison: We like blue/green best!

* Sit in a circle to discuss a theme in more detail, speaking to each other in turn. The practitioners should sit beside each other in order to lead the game. If your theme is drinks, after talking about drinks as a group, begin by saying to the practitioner beside you: I like coffee, do you? The adult could reply with either: Yes I like coffee and I like lemonade or No, I don't like coffee, but I like tea. The next adult should then say either: Yes, I like tea and I like milkshakes or No, I don't like tea, but I like apple juice. The children should be supported to continue the game in this way, each listening to the person beside them in the circle and then turning to the person on the other side to say which drinks they like and dislike.

* Suggest a comparison, such as: I think cats are nicer than dogs. Ask each adult and child to agree or disagree: Yes, I think cats are nicer than dogs or No, I think dogs are nicer than cats. Emphasise that no personal opinion can be wrong and everybody must respect each other's views. If some children choose to say that they think both cats and dogs are nice or that they do not like either, they are demonstrating an even greater understanding and more developed independent speech skills.

Learning opportunities linked to Early Learning Goals

(See pages 8–13 for abbreviations.)
* CL–U: 2, 4, 5, 8, 11
* CL–S: 1, 3, 6, 13, 16, 18
* PSED–MR: 3, 5, 10
* PSED–SCSA: 1, 2, 8, 9
* PSED–MFB: 1, 6, 9
* UW–PC: 5, 6

Give me an answer

Equipment and resources

A large clear space with a safe ground or floor surface for movement. One practitioner to lead the game and more practitioners to participate and support the children.

Activity

* Gather the children and adults to sit as a group and explain that you will ask questions and they should listen carefully and be ready to jump up and give answers. Begin with some simple examples, such as: Who is a girl? Who is a boy? Who is two? Who is three? For these questions, the appropriate children should stand up and reply: I am! then sit down again. If practitioners need to demonstrate the game first, you could use the girl and boy questions, along with Who is older than three? Remind the players that they should sit down again after giving each answer and be ready to listen to the next question.

* Gradually increase the complexity of the questions. For example: Who has a baby at home? Whose house has stairs in it? Whose car is blue? Whose brother is bigger than them? Who likes cheese sandwiches? Some children will only be able to manage the listening and the standing up and some will only be able to answer Me! each time, but encourage those children who are ready to formulate correct and appropriate answers, such as: I have one. My house does. Our car is. My brother is. I like them.

Extensions

* Include other instructions as well as questions, instead of just standing up. If you make them appropriate and amusing, the children will manage them. For example: If you have a cat at home, creep like a cat and say meow! If you like toast, show me how you munch it up!

* Ask open-ended questions and invite children to think of answers and then jump up and shout out their ideas. Practitioners may need to model this at first, until they understand and gain in confidence. For example: What could you do at the seaside? Build sandcastles! Paddle in the sea! Fly a kite! Dig a hole! Eat an ice cream!

* Invite players to stand in a large circle and take turns to stand up one by one and individually offer their answers to a creative question. For example: What would you like to paint a picture of? Answers could range from simple ideas, such as My house, to flights of fantasy, such as The den where the dragons sleep after they've collected all their jewels and made special nests. Support and encourage any children who struggle to think of a relevant answer and praise and value all contributions.

Learning opportunities linked to Early Learning Goals

(See pages 8–13 for abbreviations.)
* CL–LA: 9, 10,11
* CL–U: 4, 5, 8
* CL–S: 1, 3, 5
* PSED–MR: 2, 7
* PSED–SCSA: 1, 3, 6
* PD–MH: 2
* EAD–EUMM: 1
* UW–PC: 2, 7

Count the beats

Equipment and resources

A large clear space with a safe ground or floor surface for movement. One practitioner to lead the game and more practitioners to participate and support the children. A musical instrument that can make a clear and definite sound in separate beats, such as a drum or a handbell.

Activity

* Gather the children and adults to sit as a group and demonstrate the instrument and its sound. Play one beat, two beats, three beats and so on, up to ten beats, counting aloud as you make each sound. Repeat the exercise and invite the children to count along with you.

* Play a random number of beats and ask the children to count in their heads and call out to tell you how many beats when you stop playing. Repeat with different numbers between one and ten, until you have covered each number several times. Note which children can manage this task easily, which understand the concept and can cope with the smaller numbers and which have not yet grasped the idea.

Extensions

* Invite children to hold up the correct number of fingers after each number of beats, instead of calling out a number. This allows you to see more easily which children are confident and which may be copying others. Combining listening, thinking and the coordination of hands may be harder for some children than listening, thinking and using speech. If this degree of fine motor skill causes difficulties, you could consider using tokens such as counters or marbles for children to pick up or put onto a lid or tray to match the numbers instead.

* Play two sequences of beats, one after the other. Ask the children to listen to both and then to say whether the first or second was the greater number. They could call out One or Two to indicate the bigger number, or More or Less to indicate the number of beats in the second compared with the first. (Not many children of this age are ready to use the word Fewer.)

* Try the game as a filler at random moments, to find out whether the children remember it and have grasped the concept securely. Ring the front doorbell a number of times while waiting for a group of children to be ready to go out on a trip, inviting those already waiting in a line to count the rings. Encourage children to count the number of times the microwave beeps when it finishes its cooking, or the number of times different birds call outside in the garden.

Learning opportunities linked to Early Learning Goals

(See pages 8–13 for abbreviations.)
* CL–LA: 3, 9, 10, 11
* CL–U: 5, 8
* PSED–MR: 2, 7
* PD–MH: 4
* M–N: 2, 4, 5, 7
* M–SSM: 10

© Debbie Chalmers and Brilliant Publications

Catch the ball

Equipment and resources

A large clear space with a safe ground or floor surface for movement. One practitioner to lead the game and more practitioners to participate and support the children. A soft foam ball (or a beanbag).

Activity

* Invite the children and practitioners to sit in a circle, allowing some distance between each player. Roll or throw the ball to another practitioner, using a name to attract attention and the word Catch! as you let go of the ball, to indicate that it is on its way. For example: Josh – catch! Invite the adult to return the ball to you, using your name and the action word in the same way.

* Encourage players to roll or throw the ball to each other around the circle, in a completely random order, using names and the action word. Ask them to try to catch the ball as it comes towards them, but reassure them that it does not matter if they miss it and they may simply fetch it and bring it back to the circle to continue with their turn. The adults should ensure that all children are included and taking turns as equally as possible. Offer lots of praise for good catches, quick responses and participation.

* If two or more children or practitioners have the same name, play the game in smaller groups, with separate circles or at separate times, to avoid confusion.

Extensions

* Play the game with a group of between five and ten children and practitioners and give each player a number instead of their name. Encourage everybody to try to remember the numbers and call them out and respond to them correctly as they roll or throw the ball.

* At each turn, bounce the ball into the centre of the circle and then call out a player's name. The named person should respond quickly by running into the centre and trying to catch the ball before it stops bouncing. (If using a beanbag, throw it into the centre of the circle and ask the player just to rush in and snatch it up quickly.)

* Suggest that players talk to the ball before they roll or throw it, asking it to go to see their friend or something similar. Model a speech for them to aspire to, such as: You're such a nice friendly ball and such a beautiful bright yellow, I'd like you to go and see my friend Millie please, to make her feel happy. Children, and the practitioners who work with them, spend so much time talking to and on behalf of toys and puppets, they can easily transfer the skill to inanimate objects and toys of other kinds!

Learning opportunities linked to Early Learning Goals

(See pages 8–13 for abbreviations.)
* CL–LA: 5, 9, 10, 11
* CL–S: 6, 13, 21
* PSED–MR: 7
* PSED–SCSA: 3, 4
* PD–MH: 8
* EAD–EUMM: 1, 15
* M–N: 4

Hobbies

Equipment and resources

A large clear space. One practitioner to lead the activity and two or more practitioners to participate and support the children.

Activity

* Tell the children about a hobby or activity that you enjoy. Try to ensure that it is something they can imagine and understand, such as swimming, dancing, playing tennis, walking a dog, knitting, painting or singing. Ask two other practitioners to describe their different interests. Then invite the children to think of activities that they enjoy, either in the setting or at home, that they could talk about to others. If some are unsure, offer suggestions, such as dressing up, making models, running, cooking or visiting grandparents.

* Help the children to choose partners and ask each pair to tell each other about what they like to do. Support them in taking turns to describe their activity and its sequence and then to listen and show interest while their friend speaks. Suggest that asking a few questions shows that you are interested and understanding. Offer ideas for suitable questions, such as: When do you go there? What do you have to wear? Which part is your favourite?

Extensions

* Invite any children who feel confident enough to talk to the whole group. Encourage those listening to think of questions to ask and support the speakers in answering them clearly.

* Begin to describe an activity to the group without naming it and ask the children to guess and call out what it is from your clues.

* Collect a list of the children's and adults' favourite activities and hobbies and ask how many in the group enjoy each one. Make a bar chart together to illustrate how popular each activity is within your group. This also helps children to understand that people may enjoy many different hobbies and make different friends through each one.

Learning opportunities linked to Early Learning Goals

(See pages 8–13 for abbreviations.)
* CL–LA: 6, 9
* CL–U: 3, 5, 11
* CL–S: 3, 4, 8, 9, 13, 14, 19
* PSED–MR: 8, 9, 10
* PSED–SCSA: 1, 6, 8, 9
* PSED–MFB: 5, 6, 11, 12
* UW–PC: 4, 5, 6, 7, 8, 9, 10

Name the instrument

Equipment and resources

A large clear space. One practitioner to lead the activity and more practitioners to support the children. A selection of musical instruments in a basket or box. A screen or display board or a table on its side, to form a barrier.

Activity

* Invite the children and adults to sit in a group close to the barrier. Show each of the instruments to them in turn, name it and demonstrate its sound. Do this more than once if you think that some of the children may be unsure of any of the names or sounds.

* Take the basket of instruments behind the barrier, where they are not visible to the group, and play one at a time, encouraging the children to call out the name of the instrument they hear.

* If there is one that the children cannot guess, bring it out so that they can see it and name it as you play it. If they muddle two similar sounds, hold up each in turn and play it while speaking its name, asking them to listen extra carefully. If they forget a name, the practitioners could invite them to describe the instrument instead and then guess on behalf of the group using the correct name.

Extensions

* Work with a small group and provide each child with the same instruments as yourself. Each time you play one behind the barrier, ask the children to choose and play the same one and say its name.

* Hold up each instrument silently in turn and challenge the children to remember and describe in words the sound it makes. Encourage imaginative vocabulary such as: swishy, jingly, pitter patter or tap tap, as well as the more usual descriptive words: bang, shake, ring and rattle.

* Work with the children to create a song which uses sound words as its lyrics, then play and sing it together using appropriate instruments. For example: Bang bang bang, swishy swishy, ting ting, jingle jingle jingle! using drums, maracas, triangles and bells.

Learning opportunities linked to Early Learning Goals

(See pages 8–13 for abbreviations.)
* CL–LA: 3, 9, 11
* CL–U: 1, 6, 8, 9
* CL–S: 16
* PSED–MR: 2, 5
* PSED–MFB: 5, 9, 13
* EAD–EUMM: 1, 4, 5, 10, 11, 14, 15
* EAD–BI: 2, 3

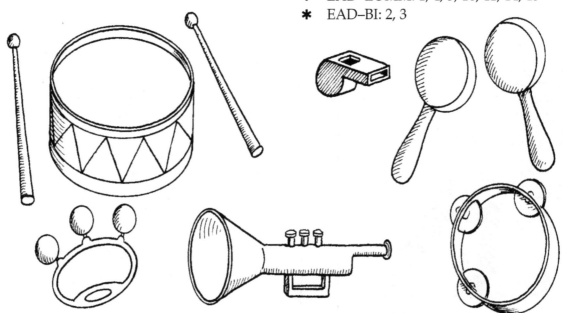

This is my story

Equipment and resources

A large clear space. One practitioner to lead the activity and several more practitioners to support the children. Favourite storybooks with appropriate puppets or toys for acting out the stories. Paper and mark making materials.

Activity

* Invite small groups of three or four children to sit in spaces. Some groups may need the support of a practitioner sitting with them, while others may appreciate support from time to time from a practitioner who moves between groups. Choose some familiar stories that are popular with the children in your setting. Give each book to a small group and invite them to look through the pictures and discuss the story for a few minutes.

* Encourage each group in turn to work together to hold up the book, show the pictures and tell the story to the other children and adults. Offer prompts and cues to help the groups if they need them during their performances. All practitioners should remind and support the children to ensure that they form a good audience for each other, listening quietly and joining in appropriately.

* Praise all children for their contributions and note which children are especially confident, who can hold the attention of an audience effectively, who can remember details or produce character voices and who can lead or work well within a team.

Extensions

* Supply appropriate puppets or toys and invite the children to act out their stories as plays, as they tell them.

* Encourage the groups to continue their stories after the books end, to discuss and decide what might happen next and tell their own ideas to the other children and practitioners.

* Support children in writing and telling their own stories. They might like to create a new adventure for a favourite character or take a familiar story and explain what would happen if a key event was missing or changed.

Learning opportunities linked to Early Learning Goals

(See pages 8–13 for abbreviations.)
* CL–LA: 1, 7, 11
* CL–U: 2, 5, 11
* CL–S: 2, 5, 9, 10, 12, 13, 16, 18, 20
* PSED–MR: 5, 8, 9, 11
* PSED–SCSA: 3, 4
* PSED–MFB: 4, 9, 11, 14
* EAD–BI: 4, 5, 8
* L–R: 1, 8, 9, 11, 12, 14, 15, 16
* L–W: 2, 6, 7

© Debbie Chalmers and Brilliant Publications

Which way to go?

Equipment and resources

A large clear space with a safe ground or floor surface for movement. One practitioner to lead the activity and one or more practitioners to support the children. A programmable toy, such as a Beebot or a Roamer. Play money or jewellery or shiny bricks (rectangular blocks covered in gold paper or silver foil) to be treasure.

Activity

* Demonstrate to a small group of children how to programme the toy, if they do not already know, then place it in the centre of the room. Ask one child or adult to place the treasure somewhere in the room (not hidden) and ensure that everybody knows where it is.

* Challenge the children to make the toy find the treasure. Encourage them to work together to pace out the numbers of steps needed and decide on the turning directions, planning the shortest route possible.

* When the toy has reached the treasure, ask the children to stand in its starting place and remember its route, moving as though they are robots who have been programmed, to reach the treasure too.

Extensions

* Make a rule that no more than five steps are allowed in any one direction at a time for the toy or the robots. The children will need to work out that they must use a zigzag route for longer distances.

* Give your robot children a variety of directions to follow, such as: jump around in a circle, hop to touch a wall, roll to the cushions, tiptoe to touch a door, run out into the garden and back, walk to a space on the carpet and sit down.

* Stand at one end of a room or outdoor area with a group of children, while another practitioner stands at the opposite end with another group of children. Take turns to call out instructions for the other group to follow, first discussing and negotiating them as a group, such as: girls take two steps forward, if you're wearing blue take one step back, boys take three steps forward, if you have short hair take two steps back, everybody come forward with one big jump. Continue until you all meet in the middle.

Learning opportunities linked to Early Learning Goals

(See pages 8–13 for abbreviations.)
* CL–LA: 6, 10
* CL–U: 2, 7, 8, 9, 11
* CL–S: 10, 11, 13, 17, 19
* PSED–MR: 5, 9, 11
* PSED–SCSA: 4, 7, 8
* PSED–MFB: 5, 9, 12, 13, 14
* PD–MH: 2, 8
* PD–HSC: 4
* UW–PC: 7
* UW–W: 1
* UW–T: 1, 3

Tell me a joke

Equipment and resources

A large clear space. One practitioner to lead the activity and more practitioners to participate and support the children. A selection of books and CDs containing nursery rhymes, nonsense poems, limericks and children's jokes and riddles.

Activity

* Sit together as a group to explore and recite popular nursery rhymes and introduce nonsense poems and limericks. Encourage all children to hear and recognise the rhymes and alliteration and to enjoy the fantasy and comedy, speaking lines and whole verses aloud, both individually and in unison.

* Experiment with changing the words to nonsense, but keeping the rhymes. For example:

  Humpty Dumpty was very small;
  Humpty Dumpty climbed up the wall.

  Jack and Jane went down the lane to talk to all the sheep; They counted four, but couldn't do more, it made them fall asleep.

* Make up limericks for children and adults in the group, using their names. For example:

  There was a young person called Sonny. Who found a big bag full of money. He bought a new hat. And danced with his cat. And everyone thought he was funny.

  Or:
  There was an fine lady called Jill. Who suddenly felt very ill. She'd eaten some rice. Which wasn't so nice. At the restaurant up on the hill.

* Encourage the children to join in as you act out the rhymes, to aid understanding and memory. Count the beats in the various lines and clap out the rhythms to make children aware of how good rhyming verses work.

Extensions

* Encourage children to make up their own rhymes for themselves and their family members. They will usually only manage two lines with one rhyme, such as: *My brother, Paul, Can play football* or *I asked my Nana, To use a spanner.*

* Introduce riddles and jokes which involve puns and plays on words. For example: What do you call ducks in a box at Christmas? Quackers! What do cows play at parties? Moo-sical Bumps. Young children suddenly acquire the appropriate level of maturity and command of language to understand these and then adore them.

* Suggest a theme and challenge all practitioners to create related jokes and puns for the children. (This game can become quite competitive and addictive!) For example: Which egg travels fast? An eggspress. Which egg goes to the jungle? An eggsplorer. Why do eggs go to the gym? For eggsercise. How does an egg feel when it's tired? Eggshausted. What did the teacher say when the egg did some good work? Eggscellent. How do eggs go out? Through the eggsit. Even if they cannot think of many for themselves, the children absolutely love this game and gain a confidence in playing with words that will be extremely valuable for their later literacy development.

Learning opportunities linked to Early Learning Goals

(See pages 8–13 for abbreviations.)
* CL–LA: 1, 4, 9, 11
* L–R: 2, 3, 4, 5, 6, 7, 10, 15
* CL–U: 4, 7, 10
* L–W: 3, 4
* CL–S: 2, 5, 13, 15, 16, 18
* M–N: 2, 4, 5
* PSED–MR: 5, 7
* PSED–SCSA: 6
* EAD–EUMM: 2, 7, 11, 13
* EAD–BI: 3, 5, 6

I wonder why

Equipment and resources

A large clear space. One practitioner to lead and coordinate the activity and one practitioner for each group of four to six children. Pictures or photographs to inspire questions and discussion. Paper and writing, drawing and collage materials. Books of poetry and nonsense rhymes.

Activity

* Form small groups of four to six children and ask them each to sit in a separate space with a key person or another experienced practitioner. Give each group a relevant picture as a visual aid and an interesting question to explore, such as: Why does a tiger have stripes? How can a window cleaner reach the windows that are higher than a ladder? What would happen if a big tree fell down in the middle of a forest? Why do cars have four wheels?

* Encourage each group to discuss the question and share their ideas, with the adult taking notes of what is said and by whom, as well as who contributes confidently or reluctantly, who focuses on one idea and who explores several options, who thinks logically or critically and who enjoys creative thinking or fantasy.

* Bring the groups together and invite each in turn to explain their question, their lines of thinking and their conclusions. Encourage the other children to listen and consider the ideas and to decide whether or not they agree.

Extensions

* Invite each group to make a book, taking their question as a title and including drawings and writing from each member. The adult should encourage and support mark making or independent writing at each child's individual level, acting as a scribe for those who wish to contribute ideas beyond their recording

skills. Display the books for parents and carers to read, then keep them in the book area for children's personal use.

* Introduce a crazy question, such as: What would it be like if cars could fly? Would it be fun if monkeys came to school with us? What would happen if people suddenly became tiny? Mount the words in the centre of a display board and invite the children to contribute their thoughts in words and pictures, to be attached to the board all around the question.

* Find poems that focus on descriptions, questions and unusual happenings. Include non-fiction, fantasy and nonsense rhymes. Share and discuss them with the children as a group. Invite them to create drawings, paintings and collages to illustrate them. Encourage those who are ready to begin to create their own poems.

Learning opportunities linked to Early Learning Goals

(See pages 8–13 for abbreviations.)
* CL–LA: 6
* L–R: 11, 12
* CL–U: 3, 4, 5, 10, 11
* L–W: 2
* CL–S: 2, 7, 8, 10, 11, 13, 15, 18, 19
* UW–PC: 5, 7
* PSED–MR: 1, 9, 10
* UW–W: 4, 5, 6
* PSED–SCSA: 1, 8
* PSED–MFB: 4, 9
* PD–MH: 1, 4, 5, 8
* EAD–BI: 1, 6

What am I doing?

Equipment and resources

A large clear space with a safe ground or floor surface for movement. One practitioner to lead and coordinate the activity and one practitioner for each group of six children. Pictures of people engaged in activities, in a book or photographs. CD player and CD of music suitable for movement and dance.

Activity

* Create groups of six children. Each group must include at least two boys and two girls and have a practitioner to support them. Invite each group to discuss and choose a verb (a 'doing word') together, such as dancing, jumping, walking or balancing, and tell only each other and their own practitioner what it is.

* With the support of the adult, each group in turn should perform an act for others to watch. First, they need to divide into two groups of three (with either one boy and two girls or one girl and two boys in each half) and mime their word individually and then together. The other children should try to guess the 'doing word'.

* Once the verb is guessed correctly, the actors should perform again, speaking aloud and pointing to each other as appropriate: I am dancing, I am dancing, I am dancing, We are dancing, He is dancing, She is dancing, She is dancing, They are dancing.

* Children who still tend to say: I are or We is or They is will correct their own speech more easily after these visual reminders.

Extensions

* Suggest to groups that they choose up to eight different verbs to mime and challenge the other children to guess them all. For example: I am dancing, I am singing, I am walking, We are jumping, He is balancing, He is hopping, She is spinning, They are freezing. Movements and absences of movement are easiest to guess, but more adventurous mimes should also be encouraged.

* Show the children pictures of people engaged in activities. Ask them to describe them by telling you the correct gender, tense and verb: He is cooking. She is running. They are playing in a band.

* Play a game with a large group. Offer the children three or four different movements, such as hopping, skipping, galloping and jogging, and ask them to secretly choose one to make while the music plays. They should say to themselves: I am hopping, I am hopping, I am hopping … . When the music stops, they should quickly find the others who are making the same movement and join together, saying: We are hopping, We are hopping … . Ask them each to choose a different movement when the music plays again and find a new group. Remind them to take care when moving around each other randomly during the game.

Learning opportunities linked to Early Learning Goals

(See pages 8–13 for abbreviations.)
* CL–LA: 9, 10
* CL–U: 2, 5
* CL–S: 2, 12, 13, 16
* PSED–MR: 7
* PSED–SCSA: 2
* PD–MH: 2, 6, 7
* EAD–EUMM: 1, 9
* EAD–BI: 5, 8

© Debbie Chalmers and Brilliant Publications

Hello everybody

Equipment and resources

A large clear space with a safe ground or floor surface for movement. One practitioner to lead the activity and one or more practitioners to participate and support the children. Greetings and key words in a number of languages, supplied by practitioners, children and families. Simple dictionaries or word books in popular languages and others relevant to your setting. CD player and CDs of songs and rhymes in a variety of languages.

Activity

* Sit together as a group and talk about the different words that can be used to say Hello. Begin with the many options in English and a sign and then invite adults and children to contribute words from their first or additional languages and practise saying them together. Listen carefully and strive for correct and fluent pronunciation. Repeat the activity with words used for Goodbye.

* Divide the group into two halves, each with at least one practitioner, and move to the sides of the room or outdoor area. Walk towards each other saying Hello in any language and accompanying the word with a sign. When the groups meet in the middle, say Goodbye in any language, accompanied by a sign, turn and walk away from each other. Repeat the movements until you have given both greetings in all the languages you know.

Extensions

* Collect songs and rhymes from a variety of languages and cultures, listen to them and learn and sing them together. Recognise and translate as many of the words as possible and ensure that all children understand what they are singing about. Invite family members into the setting to share and explain songs in their first languages.

* Learn to count from zero to ten and back from ten to zero in as many languages as possible and use different languages whenever counting occurs naturally within play or routines. Count stairs as you climb them, blocks as you build them up, jumps on a trampoline or seconds as you beat batter for pancakes or wait for a microwave to warm porridge.

* Explore which words sound similar in different languages and which are very different. Children may notice that Hola in Spanish is like Hello in English. They may guess that rose means pink in French if they know that rosa means pink in German, but be surprised that noir and schwartz mean black because the three words are so different.

Learning opportunities linked to Early Learning Goals

(See pages 8–13 for abbreviations.)

* CL–LA: 2, 4, 11
* CL–U: 5, 8
* CL–S: 5, 13, 16
* PSED–SCSA: 5, 6
* PSED–MFB: 11
* EAD–EUMM: 1, 2
* UW–PC: 5, 10
* M–N: 3, 4, 7

Speaking and Listening Activities for the Early Years

Look what I can do

Equipment and resources

A table activity involving creative and imaginative resources, such as playdough, a sand or water tray, construction kits, art and craft materials or magnets. One practitioner to lead the activity and possibly more practitioners if any children need additional support.

Activity

* Work with a small group around a table, engaged in an activity. Describe what you are doing and making, using descriptive language and a range of tenses and introducing new vocabulary. For example: I'm going to use this rolling pin. It feels smooth and hard. Now I'm rolling out the dough to make it flat. I want to cut out a cake shape, so I'm looking for a cutter. I like this one with the serrated edges because it's a circle and it will make the cake crinkly at the sides. I'll cut out a circle shape to make a round cake. If I cut two more and stick them on top, there'll be three and it will be thicker and more like a cake. But it feels cold and squishy, not really like a cake. I need to find something to use as candles. These straws would be good. I'll put four next to each other. Now it can be a birthday cake.

* Encourage the children to verbalise their ideas in the same way. Support them in listening to each other and offering suggestions to enhance the play, such as: We could swap cutters now and make different shapes! Shall we make some sausages by rolling pieces of dough? Let's put our cakes together on a plate and get some teddies to come and eat them.

* Of course, children often need to play quietly and develop their thinking skills without this bombardment of speech, but their vocabularies and language fluency can be given a boost if this activity is offered for a short time and repeated at regular intervals.

Extensions

* Initiate a project for a larger group, such as baking bread or making pizza for a snack or lunchtime or turning a large cardboard box into a castle for role-play. Encourage each child to talk to the group about what they are doing to contribute to the project.

* Collect some interesting objects, such as a pine cone, a paper fan, a decorated beanbag, a shaped sponge, a heavy magnet and some marbles in a mesh bag. Invite the children to sit in a circle and pass around one object at a time. Encourage them to explore it with all of their senses (except taste!) and to make one comment each to describe it. Support them in listening carefully to each other and trying not to repeat anything that has already been said.

* Pass around pictures or photographs of familiar objects, instead of the objects themselves, and challenge the children to describe them as a group. They will need to rely on previous experiences and memories as well as what they can see.

Learning opportunities linked to Early Learning Goals

(See pages 8–13 for abbreviations.)
* CL–LA: 6
* CL–U: 2, 4, 5, 6, 7, 11
* CL–S: 4, 12, 13, 18, 19
* PSED–MR: 5, 7, 8, 9, 10
* PSED–SCSA: 1, 2, 8, 9
* PSED–MFB: 5, 9
* PD–MH: 1, 4, 8
* EAD–EUMM: 1, 15
* EAD–BI: 1, 4, 6, 7
* UW–PC: 3
* UW–W: 1, 2, 4, 6

My letter

Equipment and resources

A large clear space. One practitioner to lead the activity and possibly more practitioners to support the children. An alphabet poster or frieze showing letters in both upper and lower case and a relevant picture for each letter's phonic sound. Plain paper and marker pen. Display board.

Activity

* Gather the children and adults into a circle or a group and share the alphabet pictures with them, encouraging them to name each picture and repeat its initial sound with you. Then share each letter, in both cases, and give the letter its name.

* Point to each child and practitioner in turn and encourage the group to say the person's name aloud and look for their initial letter on the poster or frieze. Take each alphabet letter in turn, pointing to it and asking people whose names begin with the same letter to point to themselves. Confident children may also be able to point to other members of the group when they see their initial letters.

* Children with names such as Phoebe, Philip, Charlotte and Cheryl will learn at an early stage that they recognise and write their names with initial letters that do not match the phonic sounds that they are spoken with. Those with initial sound blends, such as Barbara and Arthur, or letter names, such as Isaac and Amy, will learn that letters can make a variety of sounds.

* All children benefit from learning both the names and the phonic sounds for letters and some common blends from an early age, as they will need to use a combination of all these methods in order to work out words when they begin to learn to read.

Extensions

* Ask each child and practitioner in turn to think of an animal that begins with the same phonic sound as his or her name. Allow everybody to help out with suggestions whenever somebody is stuck. Write each word clearly on the paper, attached to the board where all can see it. Comment with the children on which use the same letter, such as Sally and seal, and which sound as if they should but actually do not, such as Kerry and cat or Ciara and kettle.

* Hold up objects, such as a teddy, a book, a (plastic) knife, a magnet, a leaf, a (toy) knight, a stone, a key, a cup, a photograph and a pencil, and ask the children to call out the initial phonic sounds. Then ask them to match the sounds to the letters and find out which of these words do have the initials they would expect and which do not.

* Play a guessing game on a theme such as fruit, colours or vehicles. Ask who can think of: a fruit beginning with 'b' that is long and yellow or something we can ride in, beginning with 't', that goes on a track.

Learning opportunities linked to Early Learning Goals

(See pages 8–13 for abbreviations.)

* CL–LA: 3, 9, 11
* CL–U: 1, 4, 5, 11
* CL–S: 14, 18
* PSED–MR: 5, 7, 10
* PSED–SCSA: 7, 8
* PSED–MFB: 5, 6
* EAD–BI: 7
* L–R: 12, 17
* L–W: 4, 5

Activities index

All of the activities can be made relevant to many different themes and used in many different situations, so, whatever concept you would like your children to understand and whichever skills you would like to help them develop, you can find a variety of suggestions within this book. Activities are listed here by title in alphabetical order.